DUNCAN WOOLRIDGE

ENNEAGRAM

A Comprehensive Guide to
Self-Discovery and Personal Growth
(2024)

Copyright © 2024 by Duncan Woolridge

All rights reserved. No part of this publication may be reproduced, stored or transmitted in any form or by any means, electronic, mechanical, photocopying, recording, scanning, or otherwise without written permission from the publisher. It is illegal to copy this book, post it to a website, or distribute it by any other means without permission.

First edition

This book was professionally typeset on Reedsy.
Find out more at reedsy.com

Contents

	Introduction	v
1	Essence and Personality	1
2	9 Types of Personality	7
3	Enneagram Type 1: Perfectionist/Reformer	13
4	Enneagram Type 2 The Helper/Giver	19
5	Enneagram Type 3 The Achiever/Performer	24
6	Enneagram Type 4 The Individualist/Romantic	28
7	Enneagram Type 5 The Investigator/Observer	30
8	Enneagram Type 6 The Loyalist	32
9	Enneagram Type 7 The Enthusiast/ Adventurer	38
10	Enneagram Type 8 The Challenger/Asserter	43
11	Enneagram Type 9 The Peacemaker/Mediator	47
12	Enneagram Test	50
13	Enneagram's Arrows	54
14	A Guide to Spiritual Transformation	60
15	Becoming Spiritually Alive	62
16	Embrace your Growth	67
17	Change to Growth	73
18	How to Have Happier and Stronger Relationships	76
19	The Triads, the Heart and Soul of the Enneagram	79
20	Discover Who you are and Who you can Be	82
21	The Enneagram Effect	86
22	Benefits of Using Enneagram	88
23	How To Get Along With Different EnneagramTypes?	94
24	Dynamics and Variations	99
25	How to Analyze People Body Language	104

Introduction

You may have experienced the sensation before—the one where you feel adrift in the vastness of the universe, sensing a place for everyone but yourself. Questions like "What is my life mission?" or "What is my purpose?" linger as you navigate the routine from home to work and back, occasionally deviating for various reasons like picking up dinner or attending your children's extracurricular activities. Yet, that feeling persists, carving a profound void within your soul.

During this juncture in your life, it becomes essential to expand your mindset, allowing you to heed the messages from the universe. When you feel lost in the metaphorical woods, it signifies the universe attempting to communicate with you. These messages are vital, and the universe endeavors to assist you. To comprehend and receive these messages, you must grasp the fundamental concepts outlined in this book.

So, what should you be attentive to, and what kinds of messages is the universe conveying? These messages manifest everywhere—sometimes in your dreams, particularly when specific dream elements remain etched in your memory. They appear in the numbers on your clock, phone, computer, car odometer, and various other places. The messages are embedded in your palm, your astrological readings, your life path number, and your personality.

Don't be concerned if terms like Enneagram or life path number seem unfamiliar. The contents of the book elucidate these concepts, including three techniques to open your mind, heart, and soul, enabling you to comprehend and embrace the knowledge to truly interpret your messages.

I, too, was once lost, but delving into my life path number, Enneagram personality type, dreams, and noting recurring numbers daily facilitated my self-discovery. While my journey continues, I grow stronger and wiser each day. By attuning yourself to the universe's messages, you'll uncover your unique life path—the journey solely meant for you. You'll experience a sense of belonging, love, a mission, and a purpose, propelling you to live life to its fullest.

Feeling lost is an agonizing experience, and I wish to spare anyone from enduring it because I comprehend its clarity. After reading this book, I assure you that you'll embark on your self-discovery journey. I believe in you, and I'm here to guide you in believing in yourself.

Reading the words in this book won't be a source of regret, but neglecting to understand the universe's signs will. Today, you can seize control of your life, or you can persist in wandering lost in your woods. Your meadow of flowers, waterfall, rainbow, and even your magical unicorn awaits, but the conscious decision to open your mind to this book and comprehend the universe's signs is crucial.

You need to open your mind to the subsequent sections, delving into numerology, astrology, angel numbers, palm reading, and the Enneagram. Simultaneously, it's perfectly acceptable to take your time with this book; time aids understanding. As you read, time will enable you to discern the universe's signs, guiding you through them. For instance, if you consistently encounter "3:33" on the clock, the angel numbers section can elucidate its meaning and guide your next steps. The book aims not only to assist you but to instill a habit that automatically recognizes the signs, making them apparent without conscious effort. The universe places them before you, and you intuitively acknowledge, "Ah yes, there's my message."

1

Essence and Personality

The term 'Enneagram' originates from Greek, with 'ennea' meaning nine and 'gram' referring to a written thing. Each point on the Enneagram symbolizes a unique personality type labeled as "Type 1," "Type 2," "Type 3," and so on. Initial encounters with the Enneagram often result in confusion between types and numbers. Consequently, individuals commonly use nicknames that encapsulate a key trait of the respective personality type.

The nine Enneagram types and their corresponding nicknames are as follows:
  - Type 1: the Reformer; the Perfectionist
  - Type 2: the Helper
  - Type 3: the Achiever; the Performer
  - Type 4: the Individualist; the Romantic
  - Type 5: the Observer; the Investigator
  - Type 6: the Loyalist; the Skeptic
  - Type 7: the Enthusiast
  - Type 8: the Challenger; the Protector
  - Type 9: the Peacemaker

Understanding each Enneagram type often becomes clearer when identifying a family member or friend embodying that personality type. Abstract concepts related to a mysterious "Three" or "Seven" gain clarity when associated with a specific person. To simplify the process, we assign a name to each personality type right away. As we introduce each Enneagram type, we will concurrently present a character representing that personality type. Brief scenarios will offer context, making the personality types relatable and providing insights into how each one experiences the world.

As we progress through each Enneagram point, you'll meet characters like Susan (a Two), Alison (a Three), Jennifer (another Three), Markus (a Four), Peter (a Five), Jane (a Six), Dirk (a Seven), Dana (an Eight), Sophie (a Nine), and Henry (a One).

You may question why we start with Two and end with One. If you haven't considered this, please bear with us for a moment. A convenient way to categorize the nine personality types is by dividing them into three primary centers of intelligence: Heart (Feeling), Head (Thinking), and Gut (Instinctive).

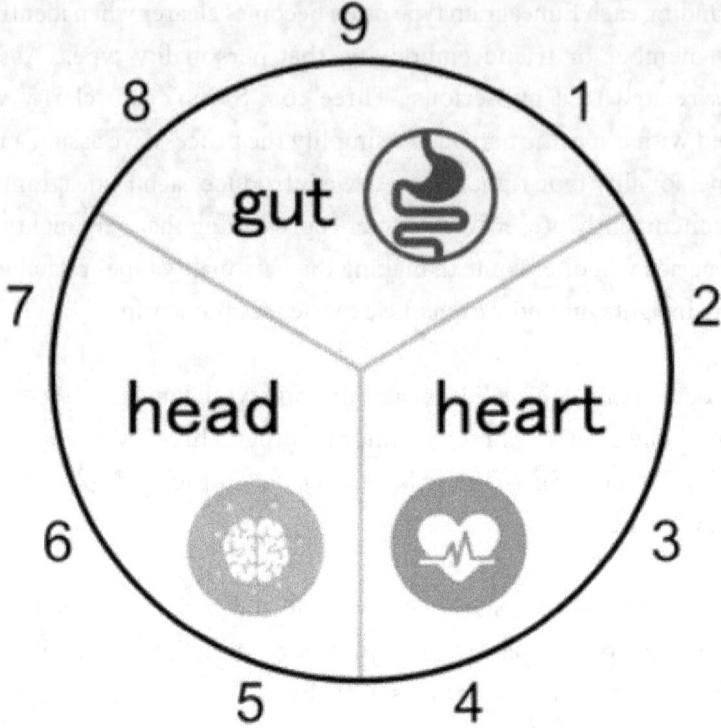

Each individual possesses varying degrees of the three centers within them. The Head, or thinking, intelligence is the most straightforward for us to understand. Whether your Enneagram type falls within the Head Triad or not, decision-making and motivation are influenced by processes occurring in the head center, guided by logic and reason. The distinction between non-Head types and Head types lies in the fact that the latter predominantly utilize their Head Center as the primary guiding force in their actions and perception of the world. On the contrary, Enneagram types in the gut center may occasionally use the head center but primarily operate based on visceral instincts originating in the gut center.

The three centers—Head, Heart, and Gut—interact and complement each other. A person's balance and health are reflected in their equal operation from each center. Analogously, envision a three-legged stool; even if one leg is slightly longer, it can still be used, but a perfectly balanced stool is more comfortable. Similarly, individuals can become unhealthy if one center dominates excessively. Achieving integration, a state of balanced use of all three centers, is an ongoing goal.

In Enneagram terminology, "integration" signifies achieving a balanced state across the three centers. While perfection is unattainable, the aim is to have a slight preference for one center without neglecting the others. To attain this, individuals must first be aware of their primary operating center, then coordinate all three for a more balanced and fulfilling life.

The Heart (Feeling) Center, encompassing types 2, 3, and 4, relates to interpersonal and intrapersonal relationships. Knowing oneself involves the heart recognizing the truth of one's identity, fostering feelings of significance and value. The heart center types seek acknowledgment and approval due to distorted connections with self and others, stemming from early childhood experiences.

The Head (Thinking) Center, represented by types 5, 6, and 7, provides wisdom through observation, thinking, and reasoning. A balanced head center enables logical assessment of the world, fostering a sense of security. When overly dominant, it can lead to excessive planning without action or impulsivity without thoughtful consideration.

The Gut (Instinctive) Center, including types 8, 9, and 1, is associated with visceral instincts that communicate information instinctively. Gut center types are motivated by gut feelings, and an imbalance may lead to unhealthy expressions of anger, ranging from externalizing rage to internal conflict or repression.

The Enneagram, a compact diagram loaded with information, can initially feel overwhelming. Understanding the three centers is sufficient for now, but further exploration into arrows, wings, and subtypes will follow. Delving into the core personality types within each center will provide a more comprehensive understanding of the Enneagram's intricacies.

2

9 Types of Personality

The Enneagram of Personality outlines nine distinct perspectives and worldviews, representing strategies for navigating life's journey. These are also viewed as patterns. The theory doesn't assert that it defines either a perfect or flawed individual. Within each personality type, there exists a pattern that unfolds in diverse ways. Take the Protector, or Type Seven, for instance, possessing the potential to employ their power and intensity for benevolent purposes or, conversely, for malevolent deeds. The traits associated with each type can be seen as coping mechanisms, habits, or strategies, capable of being developed in either a skillful or unskillful manner.

Initial descriptions of each type involve certain classifications. The Triad, to be explored more extensively later on, categorizes the fundamental drives and fears of the nine types into three groups. The Spiritual Focus of a type reflects where an individual primarily directs their attention, for better or worse. Strength represents a common adaptive characteristic, while Weakness exemplifies a maladaptive trait of the type. The Positive Direction outlines a constructive path for growth commonly observed among individuals of that type.

For example, Type One is labeled as The Perfectionist and falls into the Defender triad. Its Spiritual Focus is centered on correcting errors with a right/wrong mindset. A Moral Compass is a strength, whereas an inclination towards Error represents a weakness. The Positive Direction for Type One involves transitioning from criticality and judgment to serenity. The essence is defined as perfection. Secure Embodiment is The Enthusiast, while Stress Embodiment is The Romantic. Wings include The Peacemaker and The Giver. Type Ones, characterized as idealists, strive for truth, justice, fairness, honesty, and moral order. Despite being effective leaders, they often struggle with acknowledging their imperfections and those of others, tending to be overly critical.

Type Ones aim to act in a virtuous manner to avoid punishment. As Perfectionists transition to adulthood, they often internalize the critical voices from their upbringing, leading to thoughts of being "self-sacrificing," good, or generous. The prevalent question in their minds is whether they are "good enough." Within the Perfectionist, a constant inner trial takes place. The prosecution presents instances where the person fell short of being good enough, emphasizing their perceived inadequacies. Despite the defendant's initial defense, citing instances of adequacy, they rarely prevail in their own judgment.

Moving on to Type Two, known as The Helper:
- Core Traits: Attacher
- Spiritual Focus: Others' Needs
- Strength: Genuine altruism
- Weakness: Neglecting personal needs
- Positive Growth: Transition from pride to humility
- Essence: Freedom
- Comfort Zone: The Romantic
- Stress Response: The Protector
- Wings: The Perfectionist and the Performer

The Givers, or Type Twos, are inclined to seek relationships and professions that allow them to assist and give to others. Often found in education, healthcare, or psychology, they stand by those enduring suffering, pain, or conflict, gaining a sense of purpose and companionship. The Giver may grapple with less visible flaws, such as an excessive need for validation, rooted in a childhood marked by emptiness or sadness, possibly lacking security or empathy. Growing up, they might have experienced conditional love, needing to fulfill a role to receive affection.

Next, we delve into Type Three, also known as the Achiever:
  - Core Traits: Attacher
  - Spiritual Focus: Tasks
  - Weakness: Fear of failure
  - Strength: Leadership for others
  - Positive Growth: Transition from self-deceit to honesty
  - Essence: Hope
  - Comfort Zone: The Investigator
  - Stress Response: The Peacemaker
  - Wings: The Giver and the Romantic

Type Threes often struggle with acknowledging their own emotions. Unlike The Giver, they are less concerned with being liked or perceived as good; instead, their focus is on success and the appearance of winning.

The Achievers derive their vitality to construct their triumphs. They are individuals who excel, pursue their careers ardently, and aspire to attain a certain status. The pursuit of accomplishment shields them from truly understanding themselves, framing their perspectives in terms of victory and defeat.

Efficiency holds significant value for The Achiever, aligning seamlessly with the American ideal of the American dream: diligent efforts lead to upward mobility. Our society highly esteems winners within the capitalistic system, harboring little favor for those deemed as losers. When threes, closely entwined with the primary vice of their personality, navigate life, they essentially embody the darker aspects of the American dream.

Type Four is identified as the Individualist:
- Triad: Attacher
- Spiritual Focus: Identifying what's absent
- Weakness: Aversion to ordinariness
- Strengths: Unique creativity and empathy
- Positive Development: Transition from self-deception to honesty
- Essence: Universal belonging
- Secure Manifestation: The Perfectionist
- Stress Manifestation: The Giver
- Wings: The Achiever and the Investigator

The Romantic may occasionally direct their anger inward, feeling guilty and "bad." Shame is a prevalent vice for The Romantic, leading them repeatedly into unfavorable situations. The perpetuation of this behavior reinforces their sense of "badness." The Romantic tends to disregard societal norms and mundane rules, perceiving themselves as outsiders, fostering an elitist consciousness that promotes a keen sense of justice.

At times, a Romantic might fall into the trap of believing that fulfilling their yearning will culminate in the ultimate acquisition of their desire, leading to lasting happiness. However, they come to realize that once they possess their desired object, whether it's a relationship, job, or material possession, discontent quickly sets in as their longing shifts toward a new idealized good.

Type Five embodies the role of the Investigator within the triad of Detacher. Their spiritual focus revolves around acquiring knowledge, and their weakness lies in establishing connections. Exhibiting strength in rationality, Type Five tends to move positively from hoarding to allowing. The essence of this type is defined by awareness, finding secure embodiment as the Protector and experiencing stress embodiment as the Enthusiast. The Investigator's wings include the Loyalist and the Romantic.

Driven by the innate need to perceive, Investigators are cerebral individuals who prioritize thinking before acting. They base their actions on objective information, often displaying openness, vulnerability, and receptivity to new ideas. Commonly found in roles such as researchers, inventors, journalists, and explorers, Investigators are known for their originality and ability to surprise others. They excel as active listeners, helping others enhance their perceptiveness.

During childhood, Investigators often encounter extremes in intimacy imbalance, either through excessive closeness or a lack thereof. This imbalance can result from cramped living conditions or insufficient tenderness and affection. Such experiences hinder the development of emotional expression skills, leading to a sense of emptiness and insecurity. This feeling of being unmoored stems from a lack of security.

On the other hand, Type Six personifies the Loyalist within the Detacher triad. Their spiritual focus involves scanning for certainty, with a weakness centered around the fear of deviance and being perceived as different. Noteworthy strengths include sound logic and clear thinking, guiding them positively from self-deceit to honesty. The essence of the Loyalist is rooted in faith, finding secure embodiment as the Peacemaker and experiencing stress embodiment as the Performer. The wings of Type Six include the Enthusiast and the Investigator.

These categories are motivated by a desire for security and certainty, making them highly cooperative and reliable team players. Known as the Loyalists, they exhibit unwavering fidelity in relationships, fostering warm-hearted and deep platonic connections. Their humor is often original and witty, occasionally leaning towards the grotesque. Well-adjusted Loyalists in adulthood embrace traditions while remaining open to new paths, possessing the ability to discern possibilities and weaknesses in projects.

Considered one of the most commonly encountered personality types, the key vice for Type Sixes is fear and deceit. Prone to self-doubt, they become cautious and struggle with trust, sensing danger in almost every situation. In their worst form, they succumb to paranoia and become victims of their own fears.

Type Seven, known as the Enthusiast, is driven by the need to avoid pain. Radiant and optimistic, they exude vitality and mindfulness. Their childlike moments contrast with the challenges faced by others. Enthusiasts are full of idealism and future plans, sharing their enthusiasm with others. Childhood experiences may lead them to repress negative events, painting their story positively. Procrastination and avoidance can be problematic in their lives.

Type Eight, the Protector, operates within the Defender triad, focusing on power and control. Impressively strong, they care for and protect others while intuitively detecting injustice or dishonesty. The Eight's upbringing often involves repression and being pushed around, leading them to trust only themselves. An inversion of the One Personality, Eights internalize the message that they need to be "bad" to survive in the world.

Type Nine, the Peacemaker, seeks to avoid conflict and is part of the Defender triad. With a spiritual focus on the agenda of others, they possess a gift of acceptance, making others feel understood. Unbiased and kind, Peacemakers express harsh truths calmly and navigate deep emotional matters with power and grace. Viewed as a default personality for humans, they may struggle to understand their own needs and nature, requiring self-discovery to find their place in the world.

3

Enneagram Type 1: Perfectionist/Reformer

A man with extensive knowledge visits the British Museum in London, where a group of tourists, guided through an exhibition on ancient Egypt, is informed by the guide that a particular sarcophagus is five thousand years old. Observing from the group, a bearded man resembling Mulla Nasreddin interjects, asserting that the sarcophagus is, in fact, five thousand and three years old. This correction surprises the tourists and disappoints the guide. As they proceed to the next room, the guide mentions a vase dating back two thousand five hundred years, and Nasiruddin promptly corrects it to two thousand five hundred and three. The tourists express astonishment, questioning how such ancient artifacts can be precisely dated, especially by someone from the East. Nasiruddin explains that during his last visit three years ago, the guide had stated the vase's age as two and a half thousand years. This episode is recounted in Idris Shah's work, "The exploits of the incomparable Mullah Nasreddin."

The following passage discusses the convictions and mindset of an individual labeled as "number 1." Believing in the imperfection of the world, this person is driven to make it better. Drawing a parallel to a crusader on a warhorse, the narrative describes how the individual, akin to a confident crusader on a mission, strives to impose their own perspective on the world, convinced that the Truth is accessible to them. The person expresses pride in being honest and hardworking. The text also highlights the impact of childhood on the behavior of such individuals, often shaped by protective systems established during early years, presenting two common options.

● The first individual grew up in a strict environment that placed significant emphasis on morality. Even the smallest errors were identified and met with punishment, while successes and positive traits were deemed standard. Consequently, this person felt constantly scrutinized and judged at every step, leading to uncertainty about whether their actions were deemed good or righteous. Adults consistently expected the child to be flawless, resulting in an inability to display weakness or laziness. There was an obligation to present oneself as an exemplary member of society, being neat, compliant, decent, and conforming to accepted norms. This upbringing firmly set the individual on a path where they had to be impeccable in every aspect, with no room for deviation.

Alternatively, individual number 1 might be burdened too early with the weight of responsibility, such as caring for an ill or depressed mother, managing a large family, or dealing with other family difficulties. Constantly comparing themselves to others, this child often felt ashamed of their background and family. To regain a sense of security and boost self-esteem, they took on the responsibility of putting things in order. This hyper-obligatory behavior led them to take charge of situations, immersing themselves in tasks and developing qualities akin to those of a soldier. Number 1 perceived a stark contrast between their idealized view of life, often based on comparisons with other families, and their own challenging situation. This awareness fueled a concentrated energy aimed at bridging the gap. Consequently, everything became overly complicated – work and studies doubled, wishes and requirements were in abundance. From an early age, number 1 engaged in activities that left little room for pleasures, as these were perceived to begin only when duties concluded, not before.

Objectives to avoid: avoiding making mistakes.

The primary aversion of individual number 1 is towards criticism, and they cannot tolerate accusations of dishonesty or insecurity resulting from mistakes. For number 1, there is nothing more distressing than being suspected of imperfection. They are highly self-critical, attributing their perceived shortcomings to not being good enough or not working hard enough on self-improvement. Innocent remarks directed at them are interpreted as insults, leading to prolonged feelings of offense due to their extreme sensitivity.

Key negative trait: anger.

Number 1 is intolerant of external criticism but consistently engages in self-criticism, which is more than sufficient for them. Consequently, they strive for perfection in all aspects of life to prevent anyone from having grounds to criticize them. However, the impossibility of maintaining personal perfection, let alone expecting it from others, leads to persistent frustration. Unexpected disruptions to planned events, coupled with others not always behaving "appropriately," evoke internal annoyance. Although number 1 conceals their displeasure externally, clenching their teeth and maintaining a facade of correctness, they express opinions with short, abrupt, and dry-toned words resembling needles. At home, they often appear irritated, harbor constant resentment, and have a long memory for perceived offenses. Small issues, such as a misplaced slipper or a word of disrespect at the table, may trigger outbursts.

Defense mechanism: Perfectionism.

Number 1 immediately fixates on the worst result when criticized, transforming the person into a "frivolous" individual deserving censure. It takes considerable time for number 1 to revise this categorical judgment, as they rarely change their viewpoint unless the accused apologizes and promises not to repeat mistakes. Number 1 categorizes people into two groups: "correct" and "all others," with a preference to avoid involvement with the latter.

Number 1 consistently compares themselves with others to gauge their progress. Success triggers feelings of worthlessness and failure, leading to a strong sense of inferiority and potential depression. Conversely, if others outshine number 1 according to their criteria, they feel calmer and adopt an indulgent attitude, emphasizing mistakes and shortcomings. In such cases, number 1 may attempt to guide or model change in others, and refusing their help results in a loss of respect and trust.

Interacting with Enneagram type 1 at work or in personal life:

Number 1 tends to resist authority figures they deem incompetent. They rely on rules, established procedures, promises, and collective agreements while accusing others of treachery.

In work settings, number 1 strives for perfection, displaying prudence, organizational skills, and attention to detail. Colleagues appreciate these qualities but recognize a preference for maintaining a certain distance.

Number 1 is sparing with compliments and may offer well-intentioned advice, often unaware that it might be perceived as annoying. Their emphasis on pointing out mistakes may lead to rebellion, interpreted as aggression in most cases.

Ideal professions for number 1:

Occupations involving the body, such as doctors, masseuses, or dancers, are comfortable for number 1. They are drawn to roles requiring constant discipline of the body, like sports or physical labor.

Number 1 may also be motivated by idealism to contribute positively to the world, leading them to pursue careers in education or regulatory bodies (administrative work, police, armed forces) where their sense of morality and adherence to rules can be fully expressed.

Variations

Self-preservation Variant: Apprehension and Avarice

Individuals of this subtype exhibit a strong attachment to personal space and belongings, meticulously preserving and tending to their possessions. In some instances, they harbor an acute fear of losing their property. The persistent, obsessive worry about scarcity manifests as a form of stinginess, potentially leading to challenges in daily life. Guarding their territory zealously, they make it challenging for others to visit without prior approval or arrive too early. To justify their behaviors, those in the first subtype often resort to indisputable arguments, such as proverbs or references to the past. For instance, they might assert, "My father always emphasized the importance of saving" or "My family has always believed in living discreetly for a happy life." While these individuals may ensure a comfortable old age for themselves and others, it's crucial to recognize that the fear of scarcity persists until their last breath.

Paired Variant: Envious Devotion

At the core of this subtype's values is an inclination to devote everything to the family. Pathological jealousy plagues them, particularly when their partner doesn't fully engage in shared emotional experiences. In such situations, a torrent of reproaches follows, encapsulated by the principle: "If I sacrifice everything for us, why aren't you doing the same?" The need for independence and personal space unsettles these individuals, compelling them to compensate through heightened emotional expressions. While they demand loyalty, any hint of infidelity after years of marriage is unforgivable. Deviation from the idealized image of a faithful partner is met with stern reproach: "I've remained loyal; hence, you must also be faithful. I don't deserve to see you interested in someone else." Whether in friendships or professional relationships, the first subtype harbors jealousy when their partner shares a privileged connection with others. Exclusive attention and preference are expected solely for them, and any diversion of time and attention is deemed unacceptable.

Social Variant: Adaptation Complexity

Individuals of this subtype strive to integrate seamlessly into the groups they belong to, both in personal and professional realms. Often, they might preemptively inquire about the people they'll encounter or the expected dress code before participating in events like internships. Fearful of being overlooked, they constantly worry that their words, thoughts, and actions might go unnoticed. Living alongside a person of this subtype entails periodic concessions and meeting their requirements in social interactions. Statements like "You can't go there dressed like that!" or "How can you behave this way around people? What will they think?" are common expressions reflecting their concern for social perception.

4

Enneagram Type 2 The Helper/Giver

This personality type is characterized by possessiveness and a desire to seek approval from others by pleasing them. Individuals of this type often prioritize the needs of others, displaying warmth, honesty, and empathy. They readily make sacrifices for others, exhibiting a giving and friendly nature. However, they may resort to flattery and sentimentality in their efforts to please, occasionally neglecting their own needs in a selfless and altruistic manner. Type Twos express unconditional love for others.

The primary fear of a Type Two is not being loved and wanted, desiring equal care in return. Ranging from a servant to a host/hostess, they are highly motivated by the feeling of being appreciated, constantly seeking approval and love from others for their gratification. Termed as the "helper," they are recognized for the significant sacrifices they make for others' happiness, measuring their success in life by how helpful they are.

At unhealthy levels, Type Twos may excessively give to satisfy their desire to help and receive love, basing their self-worth on their significance in others' lives. They focus on valued aspects of life, such as friendship, family, sharing, closeness, and love. On a healthy level, they exhibit consideration, generosity, helpfulness, and love, attracting many friends with their attractive nature.

Type Twos contribute to the well-being of those around them by providing warmth, compliments, and fostering self-appreciation in others. They make excellent parents, embodying ideal qualities—offering unconditional love, care, and support, remaining compassionate, encouraging, and patient. However, their excessive concern for others may lead them to neglect their own lives.

Other individuals with a similar personality center, such as Threes and Fours, share a fear of worthlessness and engage in activities to feel useful. Unhealthy Type Twos may resort to manipulation and pretense to meet their needs, deceiving themselves about difficult realities. They may face resentment and erupt in anger if their needs are not met or if their love is unreciprocated, concealing their true feelings with a hypocritical facade. The issues of pretense and unconditional sacrifices are likely to surface over time, potentially affecting relationships.

Developmental Stages of Type Twos

Healthy Levels of Type Two

At the initial stage, a Type Two personality is in their prime, characterized by selfless generosity and a profound concern for others' well-being. Individuals in a relationship with a Type Two feel fortunate to have them around, as they provide excellent support with altruism, humility, and selflessness.

At the second level, Type Twos exhibit deep compassion and empathy towards others. They are sincere forgivers, warm-hearted, and exceptionally thoughtful. Their genuine care is evident through a desire to meet others' needs.

Moving to level three, individuals at this stage maintain a highly positive approach in relationships. They focus on the positive qualities in their friends, family, and acquaintances, expressing appreciation regardless of the person's background. Type Twos encourage others to feel good about themselves, showcasing a genuine and selfless love. This level is associated with outstanding nurturing qualities, making Type Twos excellent parents.

Average Levels of Type Two

At level four, Type Twos seek approval by pleasing others. They actively engage in flattery to gain attention and constantly discuss the topic of love. Emotional demonstrations and over-friendliness become prevalent as they strive to showcase their good intentions.

In level five, individuals become highly intimate, often meddling in others' lives and displaying possessive tendencies. They expect reciprocation for their support, leading to mixed feelings. Despite yearning to feel wanted, they struggle to achieve this recognition.

Level six is characterized by a heightened sense of self-importance. Type Twos feel indispensable, assuming others can hardly survive without them. They display patronizing behaviors that may become intolerable to others, ultimately becoming martyrs and hypochondriacs.

Unhealthy Levels of Type Two

At the unhealthy stage, Type Twos in level seven employ guilt and manipulation, belittling others and making their lives difficult. They resort to fake illnesses and abuse medications to gain sympathy and attention, lacking awareness of their selfish motives.

Level eight individuals are coercive, expecting payback for past favors, and can be domineering. They engage in favors with the anticipation of mutual benefits.

Level nine individuals feel victimized and harbor bitterness, leading to anger-related issues and potential personality disorders. They may become burdensome to others, resulting in health problems.

Type Twos may develop certain addictions, including food, drinks, and over-the-counter medicines. They are prone to eating disorders such as binge eating, starch, and sugar-related problems, using these as coping mechanisms when feeling unloved.

Distinct Qualities of Type Twos

Strengths of Type Twos include effective communication, relationship-building skills, popularity, and a caring nature. Weaknesses lie in dependency, naivety, and a sense of entitlement.

In communication, Type Twos express empathy and support, assisting others in problem-solving. At their lowest, they expect reciprocation without communicating their needs, filled with pride and a belief in their indispensability.

At their best, Type Twos embody humility, upholding their own value with dignity. In relationships, they struggle to balance independence and codependence, often repressing their needs.

Similar to the feeling center group, Type Twos experience high energy manifesting as pressure around the diaphragm and chest. They cope with emotions by discussing their concerns openly.

To unleash their full potential, individuals of Type Two must implement the following adjustments:

1. They should prioritize self-care and attend to their own needs to ensure they can offer assistance without suffering psychological consequences. Taking breaks to focus on personal well-being and engaging in activities

that bring personal satisfaction is crucial. Additionally, acknowledging that it's impossible to meet everyone's needs all the time is essential, and Type Twos must recognize that even well-intentioned efforts may come across as intrusive.

2. To avoid codependency in relationships, Type Twos must clarify their expectations when providing assistance to others. Giving with the expectation of reciprocity can lead to frustration and resentment, especially if there was no prior agreement. It is more fulfilling to give without strings attached or to refrain from helping if expectations from the recipient exist.

3. When intending to help someone, communication is key. Type Twos should discuss their intentions with the person in question, allowing them to express their feelings and preferences. Recognizing that individuals may have specific ways they prefer to receive help or other plans with specific timeframes is important. Receiving a negative response should not be taken personally, as miscommunication can lead to chaos, even with good intentions.

4. Maintaining discretion is crucial when offering help. Publicizing acts of kindness can make the recipients uncomfortable and potentially harm the relationship. Constant reminders of the assistance given may create an obligation for the recipients to reciprocate or stop the Type Two from mentioning it. It's important to understand that recipients naturally feel gratitude when someone does something good for them.

5

Enneagram Type 3 The Achiever/Performer

This personality type is conscious of their image, highly energetic, and driven by ambition. They channel their energy towards achieving success, a goal they often attain. Individuals of this type enjoy setting and pursuing goals to enhance their skills and capabilities, earning admiration and even emulation from those around them. In positive and content states, they exude self-confidence.

The primary fear of individuals with this personality type is the dread of being perceived as worthless. They thrive on the attention that accompanies their success and become apprehensive when that sense of accomplishment diminishes. Occasionally, their preoccupation with success and the external image they project, encompassing aspects like family, a luxurious home, and an impressive car, causes them to lose sight of their true essence.

These individuals typically find it challenging to discuss negative or difficult situations. When such topics arise, they tend to sidestep or curtail the conversation. While admired, they may be seen as impatient and dismissive due to their single-minded focus on goals. This mindset also extends to their emotions, as they prefer not to let feelings interfere with their pursuit of success, often shelving or disregarding them.

The fundamental fear motivating individuals of this type is the fear of being unaccomplished or unworthy. Termed as the Self-Improvement Type Three, they harbor concerns about being perceived as worthless and not maximizing their time. Driven by status and image consciousness, they often present different personas to others and seek validation in various aspects of life.

For those identifying with these characteristics, there's an opportunity for personal and professional growth. Self-nurturing and relaxation are emphasized, advocating a slowdown in pace to observe and appreciate the world. Meditation, rest, and stress-relief techniques like saunas and massages are recommended to counteract the toll of overwork and goal-driven stress.

Acknowledging that failure is part of the journey, they are encouraged to value activities beyond work, fostering energy and freshness. Emphasizing that life encompasses more than medals and prizes, they are urged to experience love as humans beyond their accomplishments. Acceptance of preferences and desires, genuine listening without agenda, self-forgiveness, and self-compassion are highlighted as keys to increased awareness and connection with the real world.

Taking breaks, going on vacations, and leaving work behind are essential for reducing stress and maintaining a balanced life. The message is clear: strive for a holistic perspective, embracing failures, and appreciating life beyond the pursuit of success.

Work:

Recognize that your worth extends beyond your achievements. While success may garner admiration and respect temporarily, forming connections with the right people will validate you in the long term. Be mindful that projecting too much certainty can lead to dismissing alternative perspectives, hindering openness to the views of others. Always keep your ears open, listen attentively to diverse perspectives, and be aware that not everyone may match your efficiency in professional work. Choose a career aligned with your inner desires, as pursuing paths that neglect these desires may leave you unsatisfied. Develop social awareness, ensuring that success aligns with personal advancement, and compete with yourself for continuous improvement. Avoid excessive self-comparison, and be cautious not to negatively impact colleagues in your pursuit of success. Cultivate genuine relationships, find happiness beyond success or image, and appreciate the work and contributions of others. Avoid pushing yourself too hard, take breaks, and reconnect with yourself spiritually.

Relationships:

Reflect on your emotions and allow them to surface instead of suppressing them, as it can hinder productivity. Slow down, moderate your pace, and detach temporarily from goals and performances. Express happiness and appreciation to your partner, avoiding a superiority complex. Schedule family and friend time in your weekly plans, set personal boundaries on work, and be a supportive listener when loved ones face challenges. Look inward for identity, foster cooperation and charity in relationships, and appreciate small moments of connection. Resist losing touch with your true self in the quest for acceptance; invest time in discovering core values and engage in volunteer work with a pure heart. Seek honest feedback from friends, resist inauthenticity, and embrace personal growth.

For Parents:

List your children's accomplishments, share family goals, and involve them in your plans for self-improvement. Be mindful of setting realistic expectations to prevent emotional problems in the future. Encourage positive goal-setting language, keep goals achievable, involve children in goal selection, and set family goals to strengthen bonds and achieve new experiences.

Feelings:

Speak the truth, express genuine feelings, and stand up for your values. Avoid doing things just to meet others' expectations; instead, prioritize what you value the most. Foster self-awareness, and be true to yourself without hiding your authentic self.

6

Enneagram Type 4 The Individualist/Romantic

The Individualist possesses a heightened awareness of their emotions, being particularly sensitive and often perceived as the most emotionally intense personality type. This intensity may sometimes feel overwhelming, leading them to withdraw from societal interactions. Despite the common misconception of type fours as antisocial, they actually require more solitary moments than other personalities. The absorption of others' emotions can create an emotional and mental imbalance, necessitating time for introspection to restore equilibrium. To achieve this balance, it is crucial for them to release negativity and embrace positivity.

Individualists typically maintain a small circle of friends and may find their soulmate, yet a persistent fear of being misunderstood may make them feel perpetually alone. The reluctance to openly discuss their emotions, rooted in shame, further propels their withdrawal from society, fostering a sense of loneliness. When this isolation deepens, an Individualist in an unhealthy state may succumb to depression.

The dominant emotion for a type four is fear, primarily centered around the dread of making mistakes in front of others. This fear restricts their social engagements due to the constant worry of being judged. Consequently, they grapple with low self-esteem, questioning their abilities even after successful endeavors. This self-doubt is exemplified in scenarios such as an artist Individualist displaying their work at a community art show; despite receiving praise and selling paintings, they remain anxious about the possibility of disappointing others in the future.

The core desire of a type four is to establish a sense of identity. They fear being lost in the crowd, yearning to be remembered for something meaningful. The realization of a unique identity brings happiness and contentment, allowing them to stand out and shine despite their inherent shyness.

In times of stress, an Individualist tends to exhibit traits of personality type two, becoming overly involved. Conversely, in moments of growth, they align with type one, fostering the development of self-discipline.

Within the subtypes, the social category is characterized by shame, wherein Individualists seek reassurance that they contribute to society. The self-preservation category embodies tenacity, with type fours viewing struggles as transformative experiences that make them better individuals. In one-on-one relationships, the competition arises as Individualists strive to prove their self-worth, demanding recognition for their uniqueness.

The levels of development delineate a spectrum from the healthiest to the most unhealthy states. At their best, Individualists channel creativity to overcome challenges and inspire others. In the lowest healthy state, they remain honest and emotionally robust, using humor as a coping mechanism. However, at the highest unhealthy level, they experience extreme alienation, culminating in thoughts of self-harm and the manifestation of personality disorders.

7

Enneagram Type 5 The Investigator/Observer

Investigators are driven by a desire for understanding and knowledge, holding their ability to learn and comprehend the world in high regard. They are characterized by objectivity and a profound passion for knowledge and learning. Opting for a relatively private life, investigators conserve resources to ensure future independence, deeming it crucial.

Key Points to Note:

In a balanced state, investigators are mindful visionaries, adept at maintaining detachment and offering objective perspectives on information. However, imbalance may manifest as frugality, intellectual arrogance, and emotional detachment, living predominantly from the mind rather than emotions.

Investigators possess gifts such as perceptiveness, curiosity, self-sufficiency, and inventiveness. Their insatiable curiosity leads them to explore and research topics of interest independently. Often leading a minimalistic lifestyle, they may also hoard items that pique their interest or enhance their knowledge.

Rooted in a belief that knowledge is power, investigators devote substantial time to acquiring expertise. They excel at categorizing information mentally and are a go-to for answers to various questions, evident in their logical decision-making.

Emotionally aligned with introversion, investigators prioritize logical thinking over feelings. They may detach from emotions as a form of self-protection, leading to perceived emotional unavailability. These automatic defense mechanisms, however, hinder the formation of deep relationships.

Blind spots emerge from their introverted tendencies and emotional detachment, posing challenges in forming meaningful connections. Struggling with commitment, investigators find it challenging to balance support for others while protecting their resources and time.

Potential for Growth:

For investigators, growth lies in becoming more generous with time and resources without feeling overwhelmed. Focusing on engaging and teaching others rather than merely providing information enhances relationships. Addressing the tendency to hoard resources and finding a balance between alone time and relationships fosters personal development.

Balancing emotions and logic is crucial for a fulfilling life. Acknowledging and facing emotions prevent emotional detachment, leading to better emotional energy preservation in both independent and group settings.

8

Enneagram Type 6 The Loyalist

Personality type six, known as the Loyal Skeptic, stands out among all personality types for being exceptionally devoted to both their friends and personal convictions. This loyalty, while commendable, has a dual nature—on one hand, it reflects positively as steadfast dedication, yet on the other, it can lead them to hold on to strained relationships longer than individuals of other personality types. This commitment extends beyond interpersonal connections to encompass ideas, systems, and beliefs. Despite their loyalty, Loyal Skeptics are not blindly devoted; they are committed to the practice of questioning everyone's ideas, even if it means adopting a skeptical attitude, challenging authorities, or advocating for outright defiance.

Their loyalty doesn't conform to the "status quo," and their principles may defy authority, leaning towards a rebellious and anti-authoritarian stance, possibly verging on the revolutionary. Regardless of the specific beliefs held by a Loyal Skeptic, they passionately defend them, often with more vigor than they defend their own interests, even if such defense results in personal harm. This intense loyalty extends to their community, family, or social group, regardless of the potential sacrifices involved.

To comprehend the unwavering loyalty of a Loyal Skeptic, one must understand their underlying fear—the fear of being abandoned and left without support. Consequently, their primary struggle revolves around a crisis in self-confidence, where they feel insufficiently equipped to handle life's challenges independently. Seeking external support becomes crucial for their survival, whether from bureaucratic structures, political alliances, or personal beliefs. If existing structures don't meet their needs, they are inclined to create their own, investing considerable effort in their development.

Being the primary type of the Head Center, Loyal Skeptics find it challenging to access their inner guidance, leading to a lack of confidence in their thoughts and judgments. Despite their logical and reasoning nature, their constant thinking can push them toward anxiety and neurosis. This propensity to overthink makes decision-making a struggle, as they may become entangled in a loop of worry. However, they are not inclined to delegate decisions to others, as they fear being controlled. Instead, they prefer flying under the radar and maintaining a low profile to avoid responsibility and scrutiny.

The self-awareness of their anxieties drives Loyal Skeptics to develop defense strategies against these tendencies. While this can be a source of strength, providing comfort and support, it becomes a hindrance when lacking or feeble, causing a spiral into anxiety and self-doubt. To address their burning need for security, Loyal Skeptics must question what security means to them and whether it is sufficient. In the absence of contact with their intuitive inner guidance, they engage in an ongoing struggle to find stability and move forward in life.

As they search for a secure environment without addressing their emotional anxieties, Loyal Skeptics inadvertently create their own challenges. However, once they learn to resolve emotional insecurities, they realize that despite the ever-evolving and uncertain world, they can find internal serenity and courage. This shift allows Loyal Skeptics to access and share the invaluable gift of internal peace, irrespective of the chaos in the world.

The Loyal Skeptic exhibits various connected types, including the Observer

(5) and Epicure (7) as wings. In terms of security, they align with the Peacemaker (9), while their stress tendencies lean towards the Perfectionist (3). Additionally, common resemblances are found with the Romantic (Enneagram Type 4) and Protector (Enneagram Type 8).

The Likelihood of Personality Types

Alternative Types to Consider if the Loyal Skeptic Tops Your List

Considering these likelihoods, if you achieved a high score on the Loyal Skeptic examination, there's a 66% probability that it accurately reflects your personality. Nevertheless, there's also an 8% chance of you aligning more with an Observer or a Mediator, and a 5% chance of being either a Romantic or an Epicure. If you scored significantly on those evaluations too, carefully review the distinctive sections below to determine if those might indeed be your personality type. Keep in mind that a type with a strong wing of one or the other can significantly influence how the personality manifests. If you find it challenging to accept the assigned type, your emotions may be valid, or they could stem from negative stereotypes associated with that type, so it's crucial to explore any strong reactions you may have.

Misconceptions About the Loyal Skeptic

Unfounded myths about the Loyal Skeptic suggest they are pessimistic and lacking confidence, often appearing excessively timid. However, the Loyal Skeptic questions things with the aim of enhancing their life. Once someone gains their trust, they exhibit extreme trustworthiness, albeit taking more time to open up than the average healthy individual.

Adjectives Describing the Loyal Skeptic

Positive attributes include loyalty, caring, collaboration, analytical thinking, knowledgeability, responsibility, dependability, trustworthiness, and friendliness. On the flip side, there are tendencies toward mistrust, skepticism, anxiety, excessive vigilance, and posing numerous questions.

Core Truths about the Loyal Skeptic

The fundamental principle that the Loyal Skeptic may overlook is that at the moment of birth, everyone possesses an innate sense of trust in themselves and the universe. However, the Loyal Skeptic mistakenly believes that the world is inherently threatening, and consequently, all authority figures should not be trusted.

Characteristics Defining the Loyal Skeptic

Due to adaptive behaviors, the Loyal Skeptic focuses on potential issues, worst-case scenarios, conceivable threats, hidden implications, and not only observes but magnifies these threats. Their energy is directed towards challenging people, analyzing situations, testing, decoding, seeking security in strong individuals, maintaining loyalties, and championing worthy causes. They strive to avoid feeling dependent, helpless, losing valuable relationships, and facing danger.

Strengths of the Loyal Skeptic encompass fortitude, dependability, intuitive nature, a good sense of humor, kindness, a sense of obligation, interrogative attitude, protectiveness, warmth, and loyalty.

Communication Style of the Loyal Skeptic

Their communication style tends to lean towards extremes, whether excessively prolonged or rapid-fire. Regardless, they consistently ask questions, which can be perceived as either a strength or a weakness, depending on the recipient's attitude towards the barrage of inquiries.

Sources of Stress, Anger, and Defensiveness for the Loyal Skeptic

The Loyal Skeptic experiences stress due to a constant feeling of pressure when grappling with incomprehensible situations, conflicts with authority figures, and the potential loss of significant alliances. They become angered by betrayal, deception, feeling trapped, excessive demands on their time, and weak authority figures. Defensively, they react towards people who ignore them, with their responses ranging from humorous in the best case to sarcastic or outright aggressive in the worst case.

Personal Growth of the Loyal Skeptic

Their ultimate goal is to develop faith in themselves and others, dispelling doubt and mistrust. To achieve this growth, they can insist on clear collaboration guidelines, commit to timelines to limit procrastination, weigh positives and negatives equally, and check in with their fight or flight instincts. The primary obstacle is understanding how to be their own source of inner guidance and resisting the urge to stay constantly busy as a defense mechanism. Overcoming this involves avoiding dwelling on worst-case scenarios and seeking certainty before moving forward with their lives.

Supporting the Loyal Skeptic's Growth

Others can contribute to their growth by providing a reality check, encouraging them to vocalize their fears, avoiding unclear agreements, offering a reliable support system, and consistently being dependable.

Practical Tips for The Devoted Skeptic:

- Enhance your self-assurance by surrounding yourself with individuals who exude positivity and provide encouragement.
- Take note, either mentally or physically, of positive compliments that come your way.
- Embrace an open-minded approach towards various lifestyles.
- Acknowledge that making mistakes is human, and reassure yourself that it's okay.
- Cultivate the ability to find humor in your own actions.
- Break down significant tasks into more manageable segments.
- Exercise patience when dealing with others.
- Explore practices such as meditation or breathing exercises.
- Allow yourself moments of relaxation without harboring guilt.
- Engage in a new physical activity, even if it's as simple as a daily walk.

Similarities exist between the Loyal Skeptic and other unrelated types, particularly the Romantic. In the context of Romantic Type 4, both the Loyal Skeptic and Romantic share a tendency to defy authority, sometimes to the extent of recklessly ignoring rules and engaging in perilous situations. Additionally, both types experience moments of self-doubt, reaching a level that may lead to paralysis. However, a crucial distinction emerges when examining the underlying motivations. Romantics genuinely desire to remain immersed in perpetual feelings of longing or desire, a sentiment not shared by Loyal Skeptics. Another noteworthy difference lies in their pursuits; Loyal Skeptics are often focused on identifying potential issues to address and improve, while Romantics are more inclined to seek the elusive element they perceive as missing.

In the case of Loyal Skeptic Type 6, parallels with the Romantic persist. Both types exhibit a resistance to authority that can lead to the disregard of rules and involvement in risky situations. Moments of self-doubt are also shared between these two types. However, the primary distinction arises from their desires. Loyal Skeptics genuinely prefer not to be entangled indefinitely in feelings of longing or desire, a preference starkly contrasting with the Romantic inclination. Furthermore, while Romantics search for the elusive element they believe is absent, Loyal Skeptics more frequently focus on identifying potential problems to rectify and enhance.

9

Enneagram Type 7 The Enthusiast/ Adventurer

Many individuals with a Seven personality believe that everything in life is a gift, embodying a vibrant Joie de vivre that radiates through their pursuit of pleasure in a positive manner. Their existence revolves around the pursuit of joy and happiness, akin to children exploring a candy store. Sevens are inclined to keep their options open, displaying adaptability that enables them to navigate changes and setbacks with ease. These individuals are open-minded, always seeking endless possibilities and eagerly anticipating the next adventure. Unlike mere daydreamers, they actively pursue their aspirations, which keeps them constantly on the move.

However, this approach has its drawbacks, as Sevens may find themselves attempting to juggle numerous tasks simultaneously. Healthy Sevens, on the other hand, can channel their talents and skills toward meaningful objectives, achieving satisfaction in the process.

Identifying an Enthusiast, Sevens operate from the Thinking Center, although this may not always be apparent due to their dynamic and active nature. They are consistently engrossed in various pursuits.

ENNEAGRAM TYPE 7 THE ENTHUSIAST/ ADVENTURER

Key Traits:

1. Optimism – Sevens are perpetual optimists, focusing on aspects that bring joy, happiness, and pleasure to life.
2. Action-Oriented – Known for their high-energy approach, healthy Sevens don't just dream of adventures; they actively pursue them.
3. Vivacity – Sevens exhibit boldness and playfulness in the pursuit of their passions.
4. Adventurous – Always on the lookout for the next significant adventure.
5. Adaptability – Sevens, with their penchant for keeping options open, demonstrate flexibility and resilience in the face of change.
6. Visionary – Possessing visionary qualities, Sevens can anticipate an exciting future and possess the practicality to turn those visions into reality.
7. Restlessness – Despite their enthusiasm, Sevens easily become bored, particularly when faced with repetitive or mundane tasks, and they dislike being stationary.

Thinking Patterns:

Sevens often engage in anticipatory thinking, consistently contemplating upcoming events and potential possibilities. They excel in brainstorming, swiftly transitioning from one idea to the next, relishing the influx of creative thoughts. While they may lean towards broad overviews rather than delving deeply into specific topics, Sevens, though not typically studious or academic, possess intelligence, eloquence, and a penchant for sharing ideas with others. The ever-active mind of a Seven readily establishes connections between concepts, fostering creativity and inventiveness. Their ability to accumulate knowledge quickly allows them to thrive on spontaneity, generating ideas on the fly.

Sevens believe their time and energy should be directed only toward their interests.

Core Fears:

The core fears of Sevens revolve around their inner world, as they detest and fear limitations. Avoiding pain, loss, deprivation, and anxiety, Sevens keep themselves occupied with numerous options and the allure of adventure. The anticipation of upcoming events serves as a coping mechanism, helping them steer clear of negative emotions.

Sevens abhor limitations and fear being unable to explore their interests.

Core Desires:

Sevens desire to maintain freedom and happiness, avoiding discomfort by sidestepping pain and anxiety through mental and physical engagement. Their immense curiosity drives them to experience life fully, and their contagious exuberance reflects a zest for exploration.

Challenges Faced by Sevens:

While Sevens possess agile minds, allowing quick learning, their diverse skillset may make it challenging to settle on one pursuit. Commitment and decision-making pose difficulties, even in simple choices like selecting a lunch spot. Unaware of the value of their acquired skills, unhealthy Sevens may struggle with commitments and make unsound choices. The pursuit of pleasure can lead to addictive behaviors, and the constant pursuit of more may result in frustration, impacting finances, relationships, and health.

The extent of distraction from negative emotions indicates the level of unhealthiness in Sevens.

Areas for Improvement:

Sevens cram their minds with options and ideas, hindering the recognition of their heart's true desires buried deep within their unconsciousness. Their basic need is satisfaction, but the preoccupation with the future makes it difficult for them to experience contentment.

Career Options:

Sevens, often encountered in the workplace, excel due to their skills, promotional abilities, and positive energy. While they may struggle with focus on a single task, they thrive in creative fields such as art, content creation, music, writing, and travel-related professions. Their infectious enthusiasm makes them adept publicists and suitable for roles in industrial design.

Enthusiasts in Relationships:

Sevens, at times self-centered, may struggle to understand others' experiences. They work well with those who share their optimistic outlook, preferring consistent and engaging colleagues. In personal relationships, Sevens are exciting partners, but their difficulty settling down may lead to challenges. Communication is crucial, especially in relationships with other Sevens, requiring consideration of actions and emotions. Acknowledging and addressing negative emotions is vital for maintaining healthy relationships.

Engage positively when dealing with a seven. Maintaining an optimistic tone is crucial, as sevens tend to shy away from individuals emitting negative energy. Instead of dwelling on problems, focus on presenting solutions. Sevens typically avoid situations involving negative emotions but thrive on making plans. Highlighting alternative actions rather than emphasizing the severity of a situation increases the likelihood of their active participation. Keep interactions lighthearted, as sevens appreciate a positive atmosphere.

The key to resolving issues with a seven lies in compromise. Reach a middle ground and explore various solutions during discussions. When offering constructive feedback, adopt a supportive and encouraging approach. Sevens, inclined to steer clear of negative emotions, are not receptive to others venting their frustrations. Recognize that they may struggle with expressing negative emotions themselves.

Anticipate that sevens will be eager to plan new activities. Allow the enjoyment to unfold naturally. Actively listen to their ideas and convey your appreciation.

To be the best version of yourself as a seven:

1. Cultivate meaningful relationships. Find happiness in appreciating your current circumstances, without constantly seeking the next thing. Contentment can fill the perceived void within.

2. Acknowledge the inclination to pursue instant gratification, recognizing the potential for easy addictions. Exercise mindfulness to curb this tendency while making plans for the future, appreciating the beauty of the present.

10

Enneagram Type 8 The Challenger/Asserter

Engaging with an individual of the Type Seven requires maintaining a positive and upbeat tone. Sevens tend to avoid those with negative energy, so it's essential to steer clear of negativity when attempting to communicate with them. Instead, focus on presenting solutions rather than dwelling on the problem.

Sevens typically avoid situations involving negative emotions but thrive on making plans. Emphasizing alternatives and highlighting what can be done rather than dwelling on problems increases the likelihood of their active participation. Keeping interactions lighthearted is key.

Compromise is crucial when working with a Seven. Meeting them halfway and discussing multiple solutions can lead to more productive outcomes. When providing constructive feedback, offer support and encouragement, aligning with their preference to avoid negative emotions.

Sevens may find it challenging to deal with someone venting frustrations, and they may struggle to express negative emotions themselves. Recognizing and respecting their need for a positive environment is important.

Anticipate that Sevens will be enthusiastic about planning new activities. Embrace the enjoyment that unfolds naturally. Listening to their ideas and expressing appreciation enhances the connection.

To be the best version of themselves as a Seven, investing in relationships is emphasized. Finding happiness in the present, appreciating what one has, and balancing plans for the future contribute to contentment. Recognizing the inclination for instant gratification is crucial, requiring mindfulness to avoid potential addiction.

Moving on to personality type Eight, known as "The Challenger," these individuals thrive on overcoming obstacles and offering opportunities for others to do the same. Eights are characterized by self-confidence, resolution, intentionality, and confrontational tendencies. They possess enormous stamina and use their energy to make impactful changes in their environment while safeguarding themselves and those they care about.

Eights, resistant to being controlled, seek to retain and increase their power. They are often described as rugged individualists who stand alone, refusing to conform to social conventions. While they fear disempowerment, they absorb physical punishments well, sometimes overlooking the well-being of others.

Eights may distance themselves emotionally, feeling misunderstood, and have difficulty acknowledging vulnerability. Their childhood patterns often involve growing up quickly in challenging environments, fostering a need for self-protection. The survival mentality shapes their belief that being gentle or giving invites rejection, betrayal, and suffering.

In summary, Sevens benefit from positive and solution-oriented communication, while Eights thrive on challenges and resist control, often masking vulnerability beneath a tough exterior. Understanding their unique perspectives is key to fostering productive interactions.

Guidelines for the Development of Type Eight:

- While the notion of connecting with your emotions may seem like a cliché, it holds particular significance for you. Your passion is undeniable, and despite your outward strength, there's a desire deep within to forge closer connections with others. Embracing vulnerability is key, allowing those feelings to surface communicates to others that they matter to you. Striking a balance is essential – it's not about wearing your heart on your sleeve, but rather acknowledging and expressing your emotions.

- The process of grieving may be a challenge for Eights, given their inclination to avoid dwelling on sorrows. Yet, finding constructive ways to mourn losses and address hurts is crucial. The tough exterior you've built serves a purpose, and it might be worthwhile to explore the reasons behind it.

- Despite an innate appreciation for camaraderie and joyous moments with others, true intimacy requires a deeper level of trust. Identify individuals you can genuinely confide in, discussing matters that weigh on you. Open up to those you trust, and consider reciprocating the opportunity for them. Recognize that sharing your feelings and troubles is not burdensome to others; in fact, it fosters connection. Listen attentively when others share with you, acknowledging their need to be heard.

- Allocate quiet moments to rejuvenate your soul, transcending activities like watching TV or consuming food and drinks. Embrace solitude, relishing simple pleasures. Take inspiration from the tranquility-seeking Nines next door, allowing nature to restore your senses. While meditation might not be a primary choice, adopting centering practices can significantly alleviate stress.

- Balancing work commitments with personal relationships is crucial. Acknowledge the value of your efforts for both work and personal connections. However, working excessively or indulging in vices without moderation can hinder your ability to enjoy life fully. Reflect on your need for intensity and explore what a slightly less driven approach might bring to your life.

- Examine your expectations of rejection, recognizing how often you anticipate disapproval or believe you must act to prevent rejection. These feelings contribute to your sense of isolation and fuel your anger. Deep-seated anger often stems from a perceived perpetual rejection. Be mindful of the signals you may be sending that others interpret as rejection, both for their issues and as a self-defense mechanism. This brings us back to the vulnerability issue – the positive feelings you desire will only touch you to the extent that you allow yourself to be influenced.

Transforming Personality into Essence:

As Eights embrace vulnerability, repeatedly allowing it to surface, they progress toward Presence and gradually release the need to always appear strong and in control. Persistent efforts lead them to confront their Basic anxiety about being harmed or controlled by others, unveiling the roots of this fear in their personal history. Working through old fears and hurts diminishes their attachment to the fundamental wish to always shield themselves. Liberated from common Fear and Desire, a reversal occurs from the lower levels of Development. The independence and self-assertion inherent in the Eight personality structure dissolve, making space for genuine Essential strength to emerge. This transformation allows Eights to surrender to a higher purpose beyond personal ambitions. Some may even become heroic figures, akin to Martin Luther King, Jr., Nelson Mandela, or Franklin Roosevelt, relinquishing concern for personal survival to serve a greater vision. ("If they kill me, they kill me. I yield my life. The vision will go on.")

11

Enneagram Type 9 The Peacemaker/Mediator

Nines stand out as the darlings of the Enneagram, typically characterized by their lack of sharp edges and a tendency to go with the flow of thoughts, plans, or group consensus. They often project goals, values, and ideas onto others, ultimately losing their own interests in the process. Calm and compassionate, Nines willingly sacrifice their own needs, wishes, dreams, desires, ambitions, and genuine emotions for the sake of others. Despite this, they possess generous and reliable hearts.

The emotional origins of Nines trace back to childhood, where they learned to repress their feelings in turbulent family environments. Whether dealing with embittered and argumentative parents or a dominating parental figure, Nines sought peace by quieting opposition and striving for a harmonious existence. Nines became adept at mediating family conflicts, often suppressing their own needs to bring everyone together.

In families marked by narcissism or intoxication, Nines may have perceived a lack of emotional connection and felt unnoticed or unloved. Ego-driven Nines, from an early age, avoided making decisions about their own lives, hoping that others would set goals they could endorse. They believed their voices didn't matter and surrendered self-development to maintain relationships, focusing on creating a nurturing environment for others.

Over time, Nines' self-denial and constant accommodation to others can strain relationships. Despite their compliant and passive nature, there comes a point when Nines yearn for something more for themselves. They may blame others for their unfulfilled dreams, leading to a rediscovery of ambition and a desire to understand their unique features.

As the mediators of the anger triad, Nines cope with anger by suppressing it, viewing it as difficult fatigue. Fearful of significant life shifts, they prefer stability and routine, sacrificing the expression of anger for a sense of comfort. Despite their generosity, Nines harbor resentment, often expressing it indirectly through procrastination or forgetfulness. Pathological Nines, having lost touch with their own identity, live by meeting others' needs, only to face a moment of crisis when repressed anger surfaces. Some react with intense rage, while others may spiral into severe depression, overwhelmed by the realization that they've sabotaged their own lives.

Self-Realized Nines serve as mediators in the world, possessing a unique ability to comprehend and appreciate diverse perspectives, attitudes, and behaviors. They exhibit a political finesse, skillfully convincing others that they are seen, heard, respected, and valued. Nines, comfortable in the middle ground, understand that seemingly opposing viewpoints often share commonalities. With a broad worldview, they anticipate compromises that leave everyone fulfilled.

A fully integrated Nine recognizes, claims, and pursues their desires, offering their true self authentically to loved ones. These self-realized Nines express unconditional love and have transcended active attitudes, contributing abundant energy to community development.

Individuation or the self-actualization process, as per Jung, involves detaching one's identity from parental influence, becoming an inclusive personality, and addressing aspects hidden in the shadow. This ongoing process requires introspection, conscious choices, and may involve therapy or self-development.

Combining Enneagram Theory with Jungian Theory suggests that positive life experiences promote progress toward individualization and self-actualization, while stress may lead to behaviors that hinder growth. Nines progress through behaviors aligned with the Three Energy, setting realistic goals, and taking autonomous actions. Regression involves adopting dysfunctional Six behaviors, heightening anxiety and self-doubt.

Jung's personality theory highlights the constant fluctuation of the psyche between extremes, emphasizing the need for balance. Each personality grapples with its idealized self, shadow, strengths, weaknesses, motivations, and fixations. The inner and outer worlds represent the hidden traits and projected image.

A Nine's shadow conceals a stubborn streak, resistance to change, laziness, indecision, and passive-aggressiveness. Despite their laid-back demeanor, Nines can exhibit explosive rage. The idealized self of a self-realized Nine radiates peace, loyalty, patience, and acceptance. Integrated Nines contribute to a vision of diplomacy, peace, and harmony, believing in the possibility of idealized coexistence.

12

Enneagram Test

Enneagram Test Guidelines
Numerous Enneagram assessments can be found on the internet. Regardless of the specific Enneagram test you opt for, it is crucial to thoroughly peruse the instructions before completing the test. Similar to any examination, an Enneagram test is not only essential but also enjoyable and thought-provoking.

The subsequent nine sections present comprehensive portrayals of each distinct personality type. No personality type is deemed superior to others, and each depiction offers a straightforward snapshot of the respective type on the Enneagram. It is important to note that no section aims to provide a more detailed portrayal of a particular type compared to others.

Carefully read each description and identify three paragraphs that resonate most with your individual personality. Once you have pinpointed these three paragraphs, assign them numerical rankings based on their fittingness to your personality, with the most accurate description being ranked 1 and the least fitting as 3. These three paragraphs are likely to significantly contribute to defining your personality.

Recognize that while each of the nine descriptions may share some similarities with you, only select the three that align most closely with your characteristics. Evaluate each paragraph as a whole instead of dismissing it based on a single sentence. Before making a selection, ask yourself, "Does this paragraph better describe me than the others?"

Choosing three paragraphs may prove challenging. In such instances, contemplate what a close friend might say when describing you. Keep in mind that personality patterns often become evident in adult life.

To document your choices, once you have comprehended and selected the three paragraphs that best depict you, record them as your first, second, and third choices. Consult the provided answers to ascertain the personality type represented in each selected paragraph.

Enneagram Test

The following are descriptions of the nine fundamental personality types in the Enneagram.

A. I engage with matters important to me using a decisive approach, emphasizing strength, honesty, and reliability. My trust is not easily given; individuals must demonstrate dependability before I can rely on them. I prefer direct communication and can discern when someone is being deceptive or manipulative. Understanding the reasons behind people's weaknesses helps me relate to them, and I struggle to follow directives from those I do not respect.

B. I uphold high standards of correctness and expect others to adhere to them. I am naturally inclined to identify and rectify issues. Although perceived as critical and perfectionistic, I find it challenging to overlook mishandled situations. I take responsibility for assigned tasks and prioritize work over personal interests, suppressing my own desires for the sake of completing assignments.

C. I effortlessly understand various perspectives and can appear indecisive due to my ability to see both sides of a situation. While this trait allows me to mediate conflicts, it also makes me aware of differences in priorities and agendas. I tend to agree with the majority to avoid conflicts, earning a reputation for being easy-going and people-pleasing.

D. I am attuned to people's feelings and needs, often sacrificing my well-being to care for others. Misunderstandings may arise, as my efforts to understand and help can be misconstrued as manipulation. I value warmheartedness and kindness in relationships, and I become demanding and emotional if not perceived as such.

E. Driven to excel, I seek recognition for my accomplishments. I take on numerous tasks and push aside emotions to stay productive. I grow impatient with time-wasting and prefer taking control of tasks. Balancing independence with teamwork, I identify strongly with success and recognition.

F. I consider myself reserved and analytical, preferring solitude. I engage in self-reflection and value a simple, self-sufficient life. I do not enjoy excessive expectations and find solace in my inner world, free from external complexities.

G. With a vivid imagination focused on safety, I easily detect danger and have a good sense of humor. My skepticism towards authority coexists with unwavering loyalty when committed. While I desire certainty, I often find myself suspicious of others.

H. Known for optimism, I enjoy generating new ideas and interests. I invest effort in projects from their inception, but once interest wanes, I struggle to stay focused. I prefer a fulfilling life and shift focus to maintain a positive mood.

I. A compassionate individual with intense emotions, I often feel misunderstood and labeled as overly sensitive or dramatic. Seeking emotional connections, I long for belonging and relationships, finding it challenging to appreciate the uniqueness of each connection. The absence of such connections contributes to melancholy and depression.

Enneagram Test Result

Identify your personality type by selecting the three paragraphs that most accurately represent you from the options provided above. Match your choices with the corresponding personality types in the table below:

- A - Type 8
- B - Type 1
- C - Type 9
- D - Type 2
- E - Type 3
- F - Type 5
- G - Type 6
- H - Type 7
- I - Type 4

13

Enneagram's Arrows

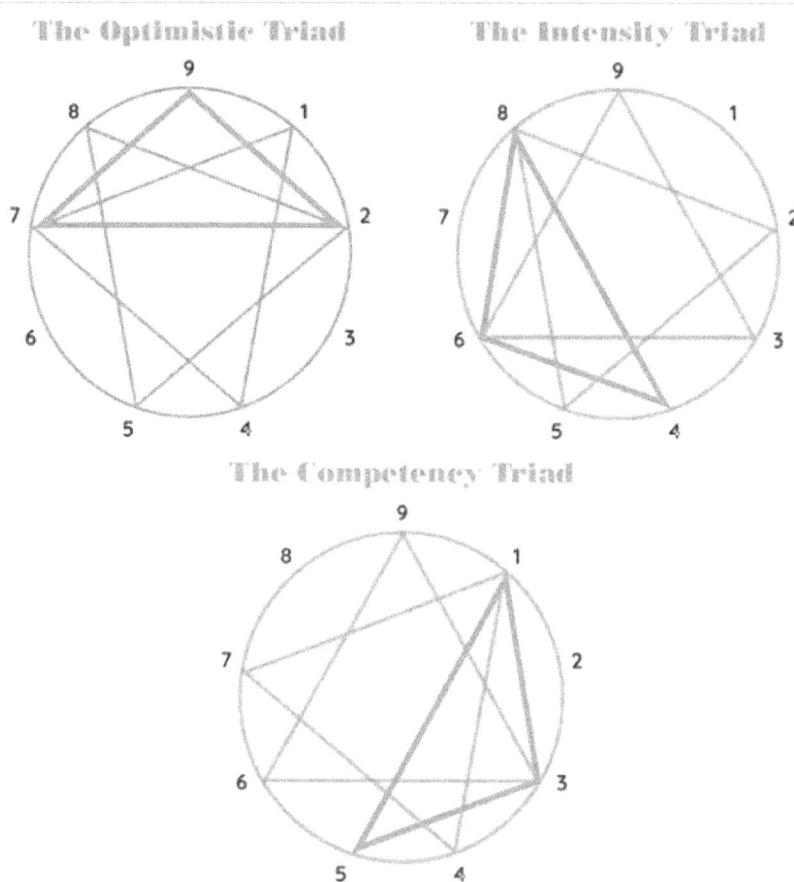

"Wings"

An additional element that can impact an individual's Enneagram type is what is referred to as "wings." Wings encompass the numbers directly adjacent to your primary Enneagram number. This permits the characteristics of the wings to contribute to your overall personality type. For instance, an individual identified as an Enneagram One (The Reformer) may draw traits from both an Enneagram Nine (The Peacemaker) and an Enneagram Two (The Helper). It is a common misconception that your wing corresponds to the type with the second-highest number in a test or the type that resonates the most with you after your primary type. However, neither assumption is accurate, as wings must be situated on either side of your type, akin to wings on a bird. Another misunderstanding is the belief that having a wing is mandatory. In reality, some individuals may not feel that they actively employ their wings, and this is completely acceptable and normal. Additionally, certain individuals may perceive a reliance on one wing over the other, a variance influenced by personal factors and motivations. The Enneagram's self-development journey often involves assimilating the positive attributes of both wings into daily life. While individuals typically exhibit a more dominant wing, the ability to leverage the favorable qualities of both wings facilitates substantial personal growth within one's Enneagram type.

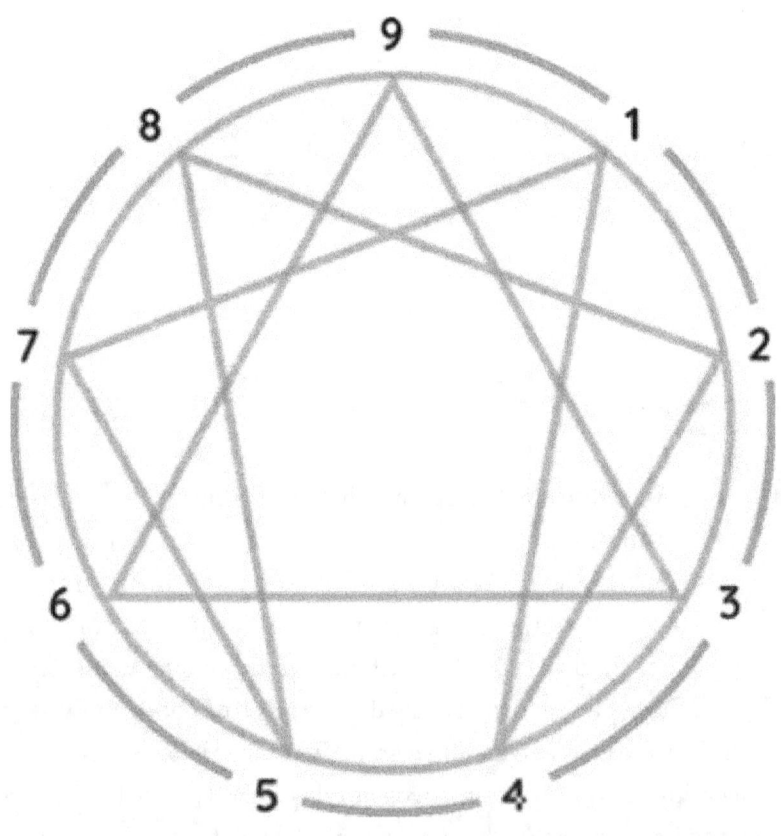

Enneagram One Wings

Individuals within the Reformer category vary significantly, as not all share identical characteristics. The personality traits associated with Type One can differ widely, akin to the diverse shades within the color purple. The analogy extends to Enneagram Ones, where individuals of the same type may exhibit distinct personality traits, much like the various shades of purple. The influence of wings further contributes to this diversity. A Reformer emphasizing their Two wing tends to be more altruistic and supportive, prioritizing others' needs and grappling with concerns about external opinions. In contrast, those leaning on their Nine wing focus on maintaining peace in their surroundings, displaying a more passive-aggressive demeanor, and possessing a heightened sense of understanding. While the aim is to integrate both wings, individuals may lean more towards one over the other.

Enneagram Two Wings

Diverse traits shape the reactions and responses of Helpers in relationships. Acknowledging the impact of wings is crucial for personal growth. A Two relying on their One wing becomes task-oriented, organized, and less concerned about others' opinions, exhibiting a stronger ability to decline requests. Conversely, a Two with a Three wing is more outgoing, thrives in the spotlight, sets and achieves goals, and values external opinions significantly.

Enneagram Three Wings

The wings play a significant role in shaping the appearance of Achievers. A Three with a pronounced Two wing appears more generous, empathetic, and friendly, whereas those leaning towards their Four wing exhibit artistic inclinations, emotional focus, and a more reserved demeanor. Balanced wings enable Threes to draw from the strengths of both Twos and Fours, resulting in a well-rounded personality with qualities like generosity, creativity, sensitivity, and goal orientation.

Enneagram Four Wings

Continuing the metaphor, envisioning Individualists as gray reveals the vast diversity within the type. Fours with a dominant Three wing, labeled The Aristocrat, are more driven, goal-oriented, outgoing, and ambitious. Conversely, Fours with a substantial Five wing, known as The Bohemian, are quieter, more introverted, reserved, and academically inclined.

Enneagram Five Wings

The interplay of wings brings excitement to Fives. A Five with a strong Four wing is more in touch with their feelings, creative, sensitive, and empathetic. In contrast, those leaning towards their Six wing become more outgoing, problem-solving individuals, but may also grapple with worry and anxiety.

Enneagram Six Wings

The wings significantly alter the appearance of Enneagram Six individuals. Leaning towards the Five wing results in a more reserved, knowledge-focused approach, while a Six with a Seven wing is generally more positive, outgoing, and comfortable stepping outside their comfort zone.

Enneagram Seven Wings

The wings distinctly shape The Enthusiast's demeanor. A Seven with a pronounced Six wing may occasionally adopt a more cautious perspective due to awareness of potential issues, while those emphasizing an Eight wing are assertive, decisive, and adept at executing ideas.

Enneagram Eight Wings

Enneagram Eight wings display a remarkable contrast. An Eight with a dominant Seven wing tends to be more outgoing, driven by excitement and adventure, while those with a substantial Nine wing are laid-back, calmer, and less fixated on always being right.

Enneagram Nine Wings

The fascinating dynamics of Nine wings become apparent, particularly when comparing Nines and Eights. A Nine with a robust Eight wing combines assertiveness with a willingness to express opinions. Nines emphasizing the One wing are more structured, detail-oriented, and focused. Striking a balance between both wings allows Nines to develop into a healthier version of themselves.

14

A Guide to Spiritual Transformation

The enneagram serves as a primary gateway for comprehending others and enhancing self-awareness. It offers insights into various dynamics and structures related to significant personality types, paving the way for a more integrated and fulfilling life. Derived from the Greek words 'ennea,' meaning nine, and 'grammos,' signifying a written symbol, the enneagram presents nine distinct strategies for relating to oneself and others. Each enneagram form represents a unique thought approach stemming from different inner motivations and world perspectives.

By functioning as a home base, your enneagram core facilitates the understanding of integration and individuation. It's essential to note that similar behavior can be displayed across different enneagrams, emphasizing that styles are not solely based on outward representations. To differentiate between enneagrams, one must delve into motivations to understand why individuals act in certain ways and why these actions hold value for them.

Identifying an individual's personality type using the enneagram system doesn't confine them to a predefined box of nine archetypes. Instead, it allows people to view the box from which they experience the world, offering an opportunity to step outside their worldview. Personality, when understood, serves as a tool for self-expression, but issues arise when individuals become trapped in automatic habits. Uncovering unconscious patterns through the enneagram enables a more fulfilling life with healthier relationships.

The enneagram model aids success in both personal and professional relationships by fostering flexibility and understanding of others' feelings and thoughts. Recognizing emotional and psychological defenses allows for profound personal growth and the improvement of one's relationship with oneself. Essentially, the enneagram enhances and expands self-observation capacity, providing a vision for the healthiest expressions of each type and guiding individuals toward a higher level of awareness.

Every enneagram type exhibits specific behaviors driven by its needs and desires. Understanding these behaviors helps individuals recognize when they are being driven by their passions, allowing for healthier satisfaction of needs. For instance, the passion of type seven is greed, manifesting in overconsumption as an attempt to find fulfillment and happiness. The enneagram empowers individuals to navigate their passions more healthily and pursue a path towards contentment.

15

Becoming Spiritually Alive

Embracing Our Authentic Identities
   The Enneagram serves as a unifying force by delineating human nature into nine variations of thought, emotion, and action, interplaying in diverse proportions. Functioning as a reflective mirror, it unveils the most genuine aspects of ourselves, providing a framework to comprehend our inner worlds. Rather than perceiving our internal experiences as random occurrences, we gain the ability to recognize them as emanating from one of three centers. This perspective fosters a profound respect for every internal movement, offering a method to categorize, analyze, apply relevant principles, and initiate transformation.

The potency of this system lies in its alignment with the truth of human nature. Choosing to understand and engage with oneself through the lens of this truth leads to a novel self-awareness. Consequently, a new reality can be crafted, one that honors and supports all that is positive.

Learning and Embracing the Enneagram
   The initial key to manifesting this new reality involves acquiring a thorough understanding of the Enneagram for practical application. Mere retention of knowledge in our minds allows us to feign learning while shielding ourselves from applying that knowledge for personal growth. While the Enneagram

can be studied as an abstract, objective system, its transformative impact on our lives occurs only when we permit it to penetrate our hearts. It is in this internal space that we recognize its objective truth and personal relevance, allowing it to translate into action and reshape our lives.

The second key entails embracing the wisdom uncovered by the Enneagram. The wisdom does not reside within the Enneagram itself but within us, and the Enneagram serves as a guide leading us to it. Loving this wisdom means applying it consistently, even when it challenges long-standing attitudes about ourselves and life.

Many individuals enthusiastically embark on the journey of personal growth until confronted with the realization that certain cherished attitudes must be relinquished for progress. Whether these beliefs are positive or negative, self-condemning or self-justifying, they become hindrances to growth, anchoring us in our current state. However, through questioning and exploration with an open mindset, we liberate ourselves from lifelong automatic patterns, gaining a deeper perspective on ourselves and life.

The Enneagram encourages independent thinking, authentic emotional expression, critical examination of beliefs, and adherence to what we genuinely know is right for us, rather than conforming to societal norms.

Living by unexamined attitudes perpetuates an unconscious, unintentional existence. To break free from this state, we must transcend societal expectations, explore new horizons, and, guided by the profound currents of Spirit, attain a fresh perspective. Only through intentional living can we collaborate with the mystery of our unfolding destiny and unleash the potential of our inherently bestowed soul power into the world.

The Third Key: Cultivating the Silent Observer

A heightened perception of ourselves and life depends on cultivating objectivity. If a new insight is gained but used for self-judgment or justification, it loses its potential to support growth. Instead, it assimilates into the existing value system that defines who we already are.

For instance, the Enneagram may reveal to Type Fours their tendency to blame others for their problems. While this awareness is brought to light, its impact is diminished if they use it to either become depressed or solidify their belief that others are responsible for their pain. In either case, personal growth stagnates.

Allowing a new insight to gently rest on our minds enables it to guide us in a new direction. For Type Fours, this may involve reconsidering the situation and identifying points where a new decision or outlook could lead to a different outcome. This is living the Enneagram, engaging in inner work that transforms the way we live.

As children, we were not taught to maintain objectivity about ourselves; instead, we were conditioned to judge and justify ourselves. These learned behaviors were deemed acceptable. Whether our caregivers labeled us as "bad" to curb our behavior or defended our actions against external criticism, we absorbed the inclination to judge or justify. These tendencies became ingrained in the backdrop against which we navigate our lives.

Judging and justifying ourselves obstruct our efforts to change, redirecting the energy created by new insights into feelings of guilt or entitlement. These emotions reinforce our existing state. To retain the transformative power of new insights, we must embrace them objectively. The objective part of ourselves acts as a silent witness, observing and recording historical events without passing judgment. This is the third key to unlocking the new life the Enneagram offers.

The Silent Witness, also known as Observing I, the Observing Self, or the Inner Observer, is inherent in every person's consciousness. However, it is often underutilized, rendering it weak. As it becomes more energetic, it becomes an agent of change, creating an awareness of the present moment and opening an internal space where alternative choices can be made.

Given that the Enneagram unveils insights meant to expose our habitual responses to life, it becomes crucial to develop the Silent Witness within ourselves as we delve into this system. Without its cultivation, the Enneagram may inadvertently become a tool used against oneself and others. Superficial exposure, neglecting a wholehearted embrace of its wisdom, and failing to develop the Silent Witness can lead to hasty categorizations, judgments, and stereotyping, causing individuals to lose interest in the Enneagram as it fails to positively impact their lives. Integrating the Enneagram into both the intellect and the heart, along with nurturing the Silent Witness, is essential for its authentic and transformative application.

Gaining insight from unexpected sources is a common occurrence, as the adage suggests, "From out of the mouths of babes…". This reality can make uncovering wisdom a challenge. The absence of wisdom can render the future undesirable since wisdom forms the foundation for enhancing the present. Hence, it becomes imperative to cultivate your inner wisdom as it serves as the wellspring of your forthcoming experiences.

According to the teachings of the Enneagram, unlocking your inner wisdom and determining your future hinges on developing the neglected center of intelligence—an often overlooked source. Personality, both a strength and a weakness, acts as the means through which we express ourselves in the world. Positive manifestations of personality contribute to favorable outcomes when the three centers are in balance, allowing the soul to radiate in daily life.

However, personality can also manifest negatively, limiting perspectives and subsequently, choices. Negative expressions arise from the misuse of the three centers of intelligence. These centers become entrenched in patterns that yield predictable results. The dominant center dictates commands to the support center, suppressing the involvement of the repressed center by undermining its value. Consequently, a restricted set of responses becomes available, and the potential for expanding one's repertoire diminishes. In such cases, individuals apply these responses indiscriminately, regardless of their suitability for the situation.

While personality is essential for navigating the world and expressing ourselves positively, it can become problematic when it becomes stuck in repetitive reactions—the compulsive dimension known as false personality or the false self. False personality encompasses unproductive and unhelpful ways of living. Recognizing and addressing these patterns is crucial for personal growth and leaving a positive impact on the world.

16

Embrace your Growth

Some individuals who are new to the Enneagram may mistakenly believe that once they identify their type, they have exhausted the system's usefulness. Although it might be tempting to think that discovering our type concludes the journey, there is more to it than that. Merely learning our personality type without applying that knowledge to self-improvement hinders our growth. By actively working on ourselves, we can break free from ingrained habits and patterns.

The Enneagram stands out as an exceptionally valuable tool for personal development because it delves deeply into our fundamental motivations. While other widely recognized personality typologies effectively measure and explain human behaviors and traits, the Enneagram goes a step further, providing insights into why we act in specific ways. Understanding the driving forces behind our behavior allows us to scrutinize deeply held beliefs, attitudes, and choices, offering a level of insight that is challenging to attain without such a roadmap.

The Enneagram also brings remarkable breadth and depth to personal growth. When utilized correctly as a dynamic system for change, rather than a tool for stereotyping and judgment, it comprehensively describes the full spectrum of our behaviors. In addition to insights gained from discovering our primary Enneagram type, we acquire additional wisdom about ourselves when exploring our connections to other types through wings, Stress Points, and Security Points.

Irrespective of cultural background and life experiences, the core psychological structure of our Enneagram type remains consistent. This universal aspect makes the Enneagram a growth tool applicable to all demographics, fostering understanding between individuals. Regardless of race, gender, socioeconomic status, or religion, anyone with a desire for personal growth can benefit from the Enneagram.

The Enneagram proves to be an excellent tool for facilitating change. Equally crucial is the self-awareness it brings, serving as a gateway to self-acceptance. Many individuals express a sense of relief upon discovering their Enneagram type. Understanding why we repeatedly fall into the same patterns provides reassurance. Through the Enneagram, we realize that our personality challenges are not our fault, gaining glimpses of our greatest potentials and gifts. This realization helps us stop blaming ourselves for our shortcomings and appreciate the beauty of our true selves, fostering self-love.

Living with accountability is a constant journey of self-improvement. Recognizing that we are all works in progress, the Enneagram empowers us to become more aware of our internal states, desires, and needs. To create positive change, knowing oneself and being accountable are key. Identifying desires and motivations discounted within ourselves and acknowledging unhelpful habits are steps toward balance. Developing an inner observer enables us to distance ourselves, pause, rethink, and make conscious choices, gaining control over our habits.

Living in harmony with our type's motivations and developing an inner observer are ways of being accountable to oneself, but it's challenging to do alone. The path to personal growth becomes easier with companions. Enlisting a partner, family member, or friend for Enneagram work provides support, candid discussions, and mutual encouragement. Finding a community committed to personal growth, whether in religious or spiritual groups or practice-focused gatherings, adds diverse perspectives and a supportive environment. A combination of personal connections and a broader group context oriented towards growth offers guidance and support as individuals connect with themselves and progress forward.

Recognizing and changing bad habits is intricately linked to the development of the inner observer. Developing this skill is challenging because we are accustomed to acting out habits rather than noticing them. Our daily lives are governed by both external and internal habits, driven by our personalities and life experiences. Our ego influences habitual inner self-talk, mostly unconscious. Cultivating awareness of this self-talk allows us to react to the immediate world around us consciously, making choices that support our lives.

As you start paying attention to your daily routines, the actions you take when not making intentional choices, you'll notice a self-dialogue in the background of your mind. Similar to your habits, this internal conversation has likely accompanied you throughout your life without receiving much scrutiny. It often resembles the voice of "the way things are." Approach it without judgment, embracing gentleness and curiosity. While your personal dialogue is unique, certain common themes emerge in the unconscious self-talk of each personality type:

- Type One: Individuals of this type possess strong inner critics, with an internal voice that may take on a parental tone. They feel a profound sense of responsibility and a belief in things they "must" do to be considered virtuous. The Ones are propelled to engage with the world based on this weighty inner dialogue of self-criticism.

- Type Two: Twos find their inner voice often focusing on others in their relationships. They concentrate on the needs of those around them and how to offer support. This prompts Twos to engage in acts of service, driven by the hope that genuine love will result from their endeavors.

- Type Three: Threes unconsciously seek ways to excel in their pursuits. They internalize their family's expectations, striving to meet perceived standards for success. This propels them to achieve in ways they believe will confer value upon them.

- Type Four: After taking action or engaging in intimate conversations, Fours promptly assess their emotional well-being. Current feelings become integrated into the Four's internal self-image, influencing reactions based on their most recent self-perception, often involving negative comparisons or idealization.

- Type Five: A Five's inner dialogue perpetually seeks ways to acquire more knowledge about a subject or situation, delving into great depth. Fives aspire to accumulate enough knowledge to act confidently in the world.

- Type Six: Described as a pendulum, the Six's inner voice anxiously swings, searching for a genuine source of safety, security, and guidance. Their anxiety-inducing inner dialogue prompts them to seek stability and reassurance externally.

- Type Seven: A Seven's self-talk tends to be extremely positive, consistently seeking the next enjoyable and stimulating experience. Their thoughts move swiftly, exploring satisfaction and fulfillment from a wide array of sources, and they respond by actively seeking new avenues for happiness.

- Type Eight: The habitual dialogue of Eights tends to amplify, aiming to sound more assertive, powerful, and confident with each thought. By constructing a dialogue filled with confidence and bravado, Eights attempt to drown out the voices of sensitivity, doubt, and the fear that they may not be strong enough.

- Type Nine: Nines engage in relatively positive self-talk ("I'm okay, you're okay"), yet it can also convey a subtle resignation to the status quo. They often imagine the pleasant aspects of their present lives, maintaining a dialogue that keeps them within a bubble of internal comfort, discouraging them from taking potentially transformative risks.

The initial step toward changing your internal habits is becoming aware of them. Through this awareness, you can consciously introduce different self-talk, gradually transforming your internalized beliefs. Changing such ingrained patterns takes time, as these habits have been part of your type's behavior for years, and research indicates it typically takes a couple of months to alter any habit.

Exploring Personal Growth with the Enneagram

Have you ever invested hours in solving a jigsaw puzzle only to discover that a crucial piece is nowhere to be found? Your initial reaction is likely, "It can't be absent. It must be present somewhere." You meticulously inspect each available piece, scan beneath the table and across the floor, and run your fingers over the completed sections, hoping tactile exploration will unveil what your eyes may have overlooked.

Walking away from an incomplete jigsaw puzzle is one thing; however, abandoning the aspiration that your life will harmonize into a meaningful entirety proves to be a more formidable challenge. The Enneagram serves as a framework for contemplating human personality and motivation, offering individuals insights into the recurrent patterns in their lives and the lives of those around them.

Many individuals turn to the Enneagram to identify the missing piece they may have apprehensively overlooked. Rooted in a synthesis of ancient wisdom and contemporary social science, the Enneagram is a model delineating the habitual patterns people employ to motivate themselves, interact with others, and confront challenges or impediments.

At its core, the system recognizes that the very strategies which prove most effective for us eventually become the fault lines exposing our vulnerabilities. Strengths and weaknesses are not always distinct; at times, the same trait manifests as both a strength and a weakness.

Overcoming faults is one aspect, but transcending strengths is an entirely different challenge. The Enneagram characterizes individuals based on their deepest desires, most profound fears, and the actions they are likely to undertake to attain desired outcomes.

Dynamic like the human experience it mirrors, the Enneagram elucidates how we undergo changes when feeling secure or stressed, navigating between different aspects of ourselves in diverse contexts.

17

Change to Growth

The Enneagram primarily aims at personal development, encouraging individuals to grow and comprehend their behaviors. While applicable to various aspects of life, such as work and relationships, its essence lies in self-expansion. Personal growth in this context involves transcending our metaphorical mask—the façade we present to the world and sometimes to ourselves. Each personality type within the Enneagram follows distinct paths in their personal growth journey.

Type 1:
- Initially, those with this personality must learn to relax and take time for themselves, understanding that not everything can be rushed.
- While capable of teaching others, it's essential to acknowledge that people cannot change overnight. Recognize the futility of forcing certain behaviors.
- Guard against self-righteous anger, avoiding alienation of those closest to you.

Type 2:
- Acknowledge that neglecting your own needs hampers your ability to meet others' demands effectively, often leading to resentment.
- Evaluate motives when helping others; ensure it's not driven by the expectation of reciprocation or appreciation.

- Understand diverse expressions of gratitude, as people may show appreciation differently.

Type 3:
- Prioritize honesty with yourself and others, avoiding the temptation to impress or inflate your importance.
- Foster charity and cooperation in relationships by slowing down and connecting genuinely with others.
- Develop social awareness, recognizing when projects don't contribute to personal advancement.

Type 4:
- Minimize fixation on feelings, as they may not be entirely supportive. Positive experiences contribute to self-esteem and confidence.
- Embrace self-discipline in various forms, from ensuring adequate sleep to eliminating vices like drinking or drugs.
- Avoid lengthy negative conversations in your imagination, focusing on the present and actual interactions.

Type 5:
- Be mindful of when overthinking removes you from the immediate experience, seeking advice when numerous possibilities become overwhelming.
- If involved in projects lowering self-esteem, consider withdrawing and evaluate future endeavors against such criteria.
- Cultivate trust, recognizing conflicts with others don't necessarily signify an unhealthy relationship.

Type 6:
- Confront anxiety directly, staying present rather than resorting to avoidance or substance abuse.
- Be aware of blaming others when upset, mitigating pessimism, and avoiding overreactions under stress.
- Build trust, acknowledging trustworthy individuals in your life and

opening up to avoid isolation.

Type 7:
- Recognize impulsiveness, distinguishing between fulfilling necessary urges and letting unnecessary ones pass.
- Listen to others, finding interest and potential opportunities in their perspectives. Balance solitude and external distractions.
- Prioritize quality over quantity in experiences, focusing fully on one thing at a time.

Type 8:
- Practice self-restraint, understanding the power of inspiration lies in caring for others. Learn to yield when necessary without fearing a loss of power.
- Recognize that others look up to and trust you, letting affection come naturally rather than fixating on demonstrating strength.
- Acknowledge reliance on trustworthy individuals and welcome them into your life, dispelling the illusion of complete self-sufficiency.

Type 9:
- Assess the need to conform to others to maintain peace, realizing that true love requires authentic presence.
- Avoid drifting off mentally, engaging emotionally and mentally in the present to prevent being swept away.
- Confront and work through both positive and negative emotions to maintain emotional and physical well-being.
- After the end of a relationship, evaluate personal contributions to its conclusion, seeking improvement for future situations.

18

How to Have Happier and Stronger Relationships

The enneagram serves as an ancient personality system capable of unveiling some of your latent desires and fears. It has the capacity to disclose insights into your relentless pursuit of something that appears almost beyond reach. This piece will delve into what each Enneagram type seeks in life, often finding it challenging to sustain or manage.

Enneagram One:
   Feeling the constant need to prove your worth and merit in life can consume you, leading to anxiety and ongoing disappointment. Strive to embrace both the light and dark aspects of yourself. Everyone possesses a shadow side, so acknowledge what feels right or wrong without dwelling on past mistakes. Forgive yourself for any wrongs committed and extend forgiveness to others. Take a compassionate look at yourself and ground in the present. What wise and kind actions can you take for yourself and others? Identify your current passions and physical needs. Perhaps, it's beneficial to sit with your strengths and weaknesses for a while, fostering self-awareness to become more integrated and less divided.

Enneagram Two:

Beware of falling into the trap of doing things for others solely for affirmation and acknowledgment. Before extending help, examine your motives. Are you genuinely concerned about their well-being, or are you seeking validation in return? Be honest about your intentions and listen to your heart, mind, and body. Avoid neglecting your own emotional and physical needs while caring for others. In your relationships, inquire about people's preferences for assistance, respecting their boundaries to prevent overstepping.

Enneagram Three:

Invest time in self-reflection, considering your actions for personal success and external approval. Find a trustworthy person to share your vulnerabilities, even though it may challenge your cultivated and self-sufficient image. Having a safe, non-judgmental confidant is crucial. Revealing your true self may seem daunting but can make you more appealing and build trust. This authenticity fosters love for who you are rather than what you achieve.

Enneagram Four:

Pay attention to your emotions and recognize when you have the tendency to intensify them. When feeling disliked or misunderstood, seek feedback from trusted individuals rather than overinterpreting every gesture or comment. Cultivate a unique talent or skill that sets you apart. Create an inspiring atmosphere in your space to encourage creativity and inspiration. Focus on cultivating peace rather than disturbance in your moods.

Enneagram Five:

Be aware of feeling detached from your body and address neglected aspects of your life, including self-care, friendships, health, and family connections. Ground yourself by engaging in physical activities like yoga or running. Connect with others daily to foster a sense of belonging. Acknowledge that attending to your physical and social needs is essential for mental well-being and reduced stress.

Enneagram Six:

Address the tendency to seek security in your environment without resolving emotional wounds. Journal about fears and worries, and identify triggers and their basis in reality. Imagine the benefits of releasing a significant portion of these concerns. Focus on daily aspects that bring security or peace, and practice living in the moment instead of constantly working for elusive security. Incorporate daily quiet time for mental ease.

Enneagram Seven:

Recognize the desire for novelty and explore the beauty in your current experiences. Instead of seeking new activities when bored, record your thoughts. Reflect on feelings, memories, or emotions that boredom may be revealing. Learn to listen to yourself and address underlying issues instead of constantly pursuing external distractions.

Enneagram Eight:

Acknowledge any childhood experiences where you felt the need to be the responsible one. Consider exploring and healing personal wounds to find balance. Examine reasons for guarding against vulnerability and weigh the potential benefits of opening up. Denying your hurts can lead to bitterness, self-reliance, and anger.

Enneagram Nine:

When you find yourself disengaging from your surroundings, analyze the triggers prompting this reaction. Consider whether confronting the perceived threat is necessary. Contemplate the pros and cons of disengagement versus engagement. Allow yourself to express anger and learn to decline tasks you don't want to do. Recognize that standing up for yourself may garner respect rather than rejection.

19

The Triads, the Heart and Soul of the Enneagram

There exist various additions to the fundamental nine types within the enneagram, enhancing the individualization of test results. This customization ensures that your outcomes are uniquely tailored to you. Apart from the basic enneagram shape, there are additional elements such as centers and wings in the diagram. The enneagram comprises three centers, broadly categorizing the nine types into three groups based on their centers. Instinctive centers encompass types eight, nine, and one; feeling centers include two, three, and four; while thinking centers consist of five, six, and seven. Identifying your personality type's center provides insights into your decision-making processes and potential threats to your mental well-being.

The instinctual center, as implied by its name, represents personality types more inclined to act on gut instincts. Members of this group are less likely to embrace spiritual ideals like coincidence, karma, and a higher power. However, they tend to be loyal and skilled at detecting deception. While they excel in intuition, relying on their "gut feeling," their unwavering trust in instincts can sometimes lead to overcommitment and trouble trusting reliable sources that contradict their intuition. Despite occasional inaccuracies, their intuition often serves them well.

The feeling center comprises types willing to do almost anything for emotional and psychological validation from themselves and others, especially influential figures in their lives. This may include parental figures, teachers, or lifelong friends. While feeling types can be vulnerable and prone to mood swings, they are valuable in empathizing with audiences or markets professionally. In personal relationships, they can be loving and considerate on good days but may exhibit wrathful tendencies on bad days.

Lastly, the thinking center may appear cold and analytical but understands the harshness of the world. Prone to depressive episodes, they may struggle with communication, as their intensity might come across as harsh and cold to others. Tone and gauging responses can be challenging for thinking types, leading to frustration. However, if they control their frustration, thinking centers can become powerful forces of logic, serving as voices of reason in friend groups and professional settings. Their analytical prowess makes them indispensable allies in various aspects of life.

Each of the three focal points also possesses a predominant emotion that becomes the prevailing sentiment when an individual within that center loses emotional control. When engaged in an argument and departing without resolving the issue, how one is most likely to feel becomes a key indicator. If the lingering emotions are anger, hatred, or intense rage towards the other person—regardless of the right or wrong party, whether it be oneself or the other—this suggests an affiliation with the instinctive center. Individuals in the feeling center are prone to feeling shame for their emotional outbursts, whereas those in the thinking center may anticipate consequences before experiencing moral weight or guilt.

Even within these three centers and their primary responses to stress, the various types exhibit distinct reactions to their central emotional theme. While both a type one and a type eight may experience anger as their primary negative response, their approaches differ significantly. A type one tends to suppress anger, channeling negative emotions into a desire for self and others' control. Conversely, a type eight is more prone to immediate and direct expression of anger, being the most likely to lash out but also the least likely to harbor such feelings for an extended period. The diversity among individuals and their inherent differences shapes the Enneagram, accounting for distinct responses within both the types and the centers they are categorized in.

In addition to the centers, there are the triads, providing another perspective on how groups of the nine basic types relate to and process the world. Often referred to as "harmony triads," these groups of three—three, six, and nine—offer unique outlooks on experiences. The first triad, known as the pragmatic triad or the "Earth triad," comprises types three, six, and nine, who exhibit control in navigating the material world by detaching themselves from or for attachment purposes. The second triad, the relationist triad, includes types two, five, and eight, emphasizing how these types contribute to sustaining relationships by caring for others and offering various forms of support.

In essence, these outlooks are not confined to the types within each triad, as they are also influenced by individual experiences. Whether one adopts a specific outlook or incorporates traits from different triads into their life and relationships is a personal choice.

20

Discover Who you are and Who you can Be

Exploring Self-Awareness

The question "Who am I?" has echoed through time, yet how many individuals can honestly answer it for themselves? Delving into the psychological realm of understanding personalities becomes crucial at this point. Self-understanding, defined as the "awareness of and ability to comprehend one's own actions and reactions" by the dictionary, prompts reflection on its significance. Many may question the necessity of knowing more about themselves, considering the various roles and titles they already carry—athlete, mother, singer, married, single. If daily life seems to flow smoothly, why bother with the potentially uncomfortable, emotional exploration of our identity?

The significance of self-understanding becomes apparent when we realize that it grants us the insight to perceive our uniqueness. Instead of simply blending into the crowd, comprehending our thought processes, emotions, and triggers sets us apart. It allows us to identify our weaknesses, fostering the ability to adapt and embrace the inevitable changes in a dynamic world. Self-understanding becomes a mirror reflecting what we already know and what aspects of ourselves still remain unexplored. Paradoxically, attempting to conceal our weaknesses can sometimes magnify them in the eyes of others.

To gain a deeper understanding of ourselves, let's explore the concept of "self" according to various popular psychological theories.

"What does 'Self' encompass? The concept of "Self" has multiple dimensions. There's the physical aspect, reflecting our level of activity, leisure preferences, favorite sports, and hobbies. The social facet involves how we connect with others, whether we prefer large group interactions, spending time with a select few, or being alone. The competent aspect assesses our ability to care for ourselves, maintain employment, pay rent, and handle tasks, considering factors like familial responsibilities. Additionally, key components of the Self include self-knowledge, self-perception, self-esteem, and self-awareness.

Self-Knowledge involves the ongoing process of answering the question, "What am I like?" It extends beyond awareness of ourselves, encompassing the pursuit of knowledge to deepen our understanding. This mental representation of individuality includes both physical traits like ethnicity and psychological traits such as morals and beliefs.

Self-Perception, defined as the way we interpret and understand ourselves, aligns with Daryl Bem's theory that attitudes develop as emotional responses to new or ambiguous circumstances. While some see behavior influencing attitude, others believe attitudes shape behavior. Approaching self-perception healthily involves acknowledging the possibility of a bidirectional relationship. Ultimately, it boils down to understanding, where self-knowledge provides information, and self-perception offers the comprehension of that information.

Self-Esteem operates on a personal level, influencing how we view ourselves and evaluate our worth, whether positively or negatively. It plays a pivotal role in daily life, affecting job performance, relationships, and academic pursuits.

Individuals may either internalize positive beliefs about themselves or yearn for affirmation but struggle to accept it, often leaning towards negative self-perceptions.

Self-Awareness is the capacity to recognize ourselves as unique individuals, distinct from others. It encompasses understanding our character, emotions, motivations, likes, and dislikes. External and internal awareness contribute to this, involving awareness of our physical body and emotions.

Jungian Self Archetype, based on Carl Jung's theories, introduces the idea of archetypes shaping our personalities. The Self archetype, symbolized by a circle, represents the core of the personality, encompassing the unconscious, conscious, and ego. Jung posited that understanding the true Self is challenging, considering it a separate entity and the source of dreams.

Johari Window, developed by Harrington Ingram and Joseph Luft, provides four facets of the Self: hidden, known, unknown, and blind. The hidden self contains aspects known only to us, often private or protected due to shame or vulnerability. The known self is what both we and others perceive. The unknown self includes aspects we haven't discovered, while the blind self holds aspects known to others but not ourselves. Gaining self-understanding involves exploring these facets and seeking feedback from others."

Understanding oneself is a crucial aspect, and delving into the Enneagram model can significantly aid in this journey of self-awareness. The initial step involves taking the Enneagram test to identify your personality type. However, the subsequent step might pose challenges as it requires maintaining an open mind and embracing both positive and negative aspects.

Fear often acts as a major obstacle to acquiring profound self-knowledge. Fear of failure, fear of falling short, fear of rejection—these apprehensions confine us within our comfort zones. Misusing the Enneagram tool may inadvertently fuel more fear and resentment. Yet, if approached with a healthy mindset, self-evaluation through the Enneagram can yield valuable insights.

The pursuit of self-improvement is a universal goal, and the Enneagram model serves precisely that purpose. While each personality type has its drawbacks, the Enneagram also illuminates the unique strengths inherent in each individual. Prior to taking the Enneagram test, introspective questions like self-description, identifying strengths and weaknesses, and contemplating desired changes can facilitate a smoother identification with a specific Enneagram type.

All individuals possess gifts and potential contributions to various aspects of life. Viewing the nine personalities without judgment as neither inherently good nor bad is crucial. Acknowledging both the positive qualities and blind spots, as pinpointed by the Enneagram, forms an integral part of self-understanding.

External factors significantly shape our self-perception, including the time and place of birth, parental influence, upbringing, and the environment in which we mature. The Enneagram model proves invaluable by offering a framework beyond these external influences. Understanding the motivations behind our thoughts and actions becomes a key to breaking free from debilitating thought patterns and habits, contributing to a more comprehensive self-awareness.

21

The Enneagram Effect

The Enneagram offers insights into both your human characteristics and your divine potential. Each of the nine universal personality types holds numerous nuances, reflecting the diversity found in people worldwide. Uncovering these unique subtleties becomes a gratifying endeavor within the framework of the Enneagram. Engaging in your inner work serves as a valuable investment in yourself and your relationships, regardless of the combination of personal growth tools you employ.

Recognizing your personality type and inherent potential marks the commencement of the internal journey toward personal transformation. True self-realization transcends mere awareness; it requires a profound understanding of who you are meant to become. Deepening your awareness and embracing this newfound understanding may open up new pathways within you. Implementing new behaviors that liberate you and overcome self-imposed obstacles can lead to profound shifts in your life.

The effects you experience will justify the effort invested in your personal growth. It's crucial to be patient with yourself, acknowledging that transformative insights may prompt immediate behavioral changes, but more often, progress occurs gradually through small steps.

The Enneagram provides practical methods for cultivating awareness and making thoughtful choices. By operating from your internal locus of safety rather than succumbing to self-created stress, you can benefit from the Enneagram's guidance. Breath work, in particular, emerges as a crucial practice. By breathing into the emotional passions that surface, you can deepen your awareness and understanding of them.

Scientific research has confirmed that with consistent practice, we can break free from habitual thought patterns and reactions. Dr. Donald Hebb's investigation of neural circuits in the brain reveals that the connections firing during specific thoughts or behaviors become wired together through repetition.

22

Benefits of Using Enneagram

The primary advantage offered by the Enneagram is its ability to enhance self-understanding. It facilitates a profound comprehension of one's inner self and extends this insight to understanding others as well. Through this understanding, individuals can cultivate greater compassion towards others. The Enneagram not only enables access but also promotes the expansion of emotional, mental, and spiritual intelligence. This heightened awareness extends to automatic responses and defensive reactions in life situations. Recognizing these reactions empowers individuals to modify their responses, as the only aspect of life entirely within their control is how they react. The pivotal factor distinguishing success from failure lies in one's reactions, ultimately influencing the trajectory of one's life. Consequently, the Enneagram contributes to increased efficiency in interpersonal interactions and facilitates the establishment of meaningful relationships. Moreover, it guides individuals to embrace the present moment rather than dwelling on the past or future. In essence, it all revolves around fostering self-awareness, a key catalyst for positive life transformation.

Confidence, the eighth personality type and second to last, is known as the challenger due to their inclination to embrace challenges rather than shying away from them. These individuals exhibit quick decision-making skills and possess a strong belief in the choices they make, earning them nicknames such as Willful, Powerful, and Self-confident. Their confidence leads them to seek control over their environment, making them appear dominating at times. Despite being influential and inspirational, challengers can come across as intimidating, as they avoid revealing any signs of weakness.

Individuals with the eighth personality prefer to maintain control, often challenging those around them to showcase their resourcefulness and skills. They seize opportunities to turn challenges into avenues for personal improvement, consistently taking charge before others even have a chance. Vulnerability is something they fear, as they strive to avoid being hurt or dominated by others. Challengers are inherently competitive, going to great lengths to win and ensuring their perceived opponents have no advantage. Their aversion to human and circumstantial control mirrors the traits of the seventh personality.

Challengers, similar to the seventh personality, dislike feeling restricted, and confusion may arise between these two types, particularly when the eighth personality's dominant wing is a seven, or a seven's dominant wing is an eight. Regardless of contradictions faced, challengers remain steadfast in doing what they believe is right, exhibiting determination to achieve their goals. Unlike the seventh personality, which pursues extremes for excitement, challengers go to extremes to prove their worth and display their strength. Stepping out of their comfort zones is embraced by challengers, as they relish the opportunity to surpass their usual contributions and excel even further.

Moving on to the topic of self-awareness, it becomes crucial for individuals to consider actions and steps that facilitate personal growth and self-awareness based on their unique personality type. Each personality type comes with distinct actions and recommendations for this journey, allowing individuals to identify what works best for them.

Advantages of Self-Awareness

Enhancement of Coping Skills

Life inevitably presents challenges, and without self-awareness, you may confront these obstacles reactively, making coping more challenging. With heightened awareness, you can navigate difficulties with grace and acceptance, facilitating a more positive and relaxed approach while empowering yourself to make constructive choices.

Self-Healing Capability

Unaddressed and buried pain tends to linger, influencing present reactions based on past pain. Actively working through challenges enables conscious actions, freeing you from the weight of unresolved burdens. The resolution of issues often leads to an enhanced sense of well-being.

Increased Internal Balance

Emotional turbulence may sometimes make you feel like you're walking an emotional tightrope, where each emotion and reaction threatens your delicate balance. Self-awareness provides strength, and acceptance further fortifies you, enabling the maintenance of balance even during internal storms.

Enhanced Relationships

Relating to others from a place of awareness fosters an enjoyable company. Unconscious reactions can lead to conflicts and heightened emotional distress in relationships. With self-awareness comes compassion for others' pain, making it easier to connect with kindness.

Cultivation of Presence and Mindfulness

Living in the present moment allows individuals to avoid being haunted by past wounds or fearing an uncertain future. Presence brings acceptance and joy, enabling a state of being where we fully and compassionately understand both others and ourselves.

Advantages of Self-Awareness

Enhancement of Coping Skills

Life inevitably presents challenges, and without self-awareness, you may confront these obstacles reactively, making coping more challenging. With heightened awareness, you can navigate difficulties with grace and acceptance, facilitating a more positive and relaxed approach while empowering yourself to make constructive choices.

Self-Healing Capability

Unaddressed and buried pain tends to linger, influencing present reactions based on past pain. Actively working through challenges enables conscious actions, freeing you from the weight of unresolved burdens. The resolution of issues often leads to an enhanced sense of well-being.

Increased Internal Balance

Emotional turbulence may sometimes make you feel like you're walking an emotional tightrope, where each emotion and reaction threatens your delicate balance. Self-awareness provides strength, and acceptance further fortifies you, enabling the maintenance of balance even during internal storms.

Enhanced Relationships

Relating to others from a place of awareness fosters an enjoyable company. Unconscious reactions can lead to conflicts and heightened emotional distress in relationships. With self-awareness comes compassion for others' pain, making it easier to connect with kindness.

Cultivation of Presence and Mindfulness

Living in the present moment allows individuals to avoid being haunted by past wounds or fearing an uncertain future. Presence brings acceptance and joy, enabling a state of being where we fully and compassionately understand both others and ourselves.

Compassion

The enneagram provides a path toward self-discovery and acceptance of one's true self. Each person possesses a fundamental driving force and a preferred set of strategies based on unique talents and strengths that define individuality. Our perspectives on the world and the current era guide us in specific directions as individuals. These preferences can solidify into behavior patterns that may limit personal growth. Initially, individuals may express a desire to change their enneagram type, indicating a judgment of one type as more desirable than another. The key to utilizing the enneagram lies in exploration without judgment, recognizing that each pattern harbors a valuable reservoir of talent. Personal growth and maturity are ongoing processes with limitless potential, regardless of one's type. Every enneagram type has its own levels of maturity and generativity, which may vary in different contexts.

Each enneagram type represents a deep-seated habit, a constant theme that often persists throughout a person's life. However, mental, physical, or spiritual development possibilities are boundless. The enneagram type serves as a fundamental form of human habit, and with technology and coaching, gained insights can be used to transform patterns for more effective behavior and perspectives.

Studying our enneagram types reveals a spectrum of behaviors, ranging from healthy to unhealthy, that we engage in unconsciously. When relaxed, we may access natural gifts inherent to our type, while under stress, our reactions may contradict our best intentions. Understanding our enneagram type enables the development of skills specific to that type, reducing stress levels associated with reactivity and quick, negative responses to others. This understanding also highlights the diversity of unconscious patterns and reactions in different contexts.

Further exploration of the enneagram fosters the development of valuable traits such as compassion and understanding for oneself and others. Recognizing patterns within types allows for the appreciation of how quickly individuals can be triggered and the difficulty in noticing these patterns. Developing skills to slow down and break free from ingrained patterns enables compassion and sensitivity to emotional vulnerabilities, creating the ability to hold space for others. Understanding the enneagram also enhances relationship navigation by providing insights into the fears, defenses, and motivations of family and colleagues.

Embarking on a journey of self-exploration is a commitment to living a conscious and caring life, despite encountering situations and people that may trigger self-sabotaging reactions. Even individuals on a spiritual path may be humbled by unconscious reactions, leading to patterns believed to be outgrown. The challenge lies in finding clarity and freeing oneself from the fears, motivations, and desires that fuel behavioral patterns and trigger reactions from others.

Leadership

Individuals categorized as challengers exhibit both persuasiveness and charisma, making them prevalent in various leadership positions. They excel in their respective fields and are often seen as exemplars of their beliefs. With a strong sense of control and restraint, challengers significantly influence society, expecting unwavering followership and opposing opposition at any cost. Trust is hard for challengers to establish, but once earned, they consider the trusted person as a close friend of great importance in their lives. Protective instincts come into play, and challengers go to great lengths to defend and provide for those they hold dear.

Challengers resist external control and fear allowing outside influences to sway them. They will fiercely fight against any attempts to exert control over them, prioritizing the pursuit of their instincts over following someone else's lead or being swayed to ignore their own instincts.

23

How To Get Along With Different EnneagramTypes?

How to Connect with Type One? Enneagram Type One, also known as the Perfectionist, is perpetually seeking ways to improve things because nothing ever seems good enough for them. This thought pattern characterizes them as perfectionists with a desire to reform and create order amidst omnipresent chaos. Type Ones possess a keen eye for details and are self-aware of their own flaws, as well as those in situations and others. This self-awareness triggers their inclination for improvement, which can be advantageous for those involved. However, it may also become burdensome for both the Type One and those on the receiving end.

Type Ones dedicate their lives to making the world a better place. Ironically, this aspiration becomes their greatest fear—that they are inherently flawed—driving them to constantly strive for self-improvement. In healthy relationships with family, friends, and partners, Type Ones are easy-going, care-free, and fun individuals.

How to Connect with Type Two?
Enneagram Type Two, also known as the Helper, derives a sense of worth

from assisting others. Love is the central ideal for Type Twos, and they strive to selflessly give to others. These emotional and warm individuals deeply care about their relationships, investing time and energy in their loved ones and creating inviting and comfortable homes. Type Twos possess a natural intuition for the needs of others and are considered the most caring and empathetic among all enneagram types.

For those interacting with a Type Two, expressing genuine love and respect is crucial. Providing specific examples of appreciation is encouraged, as Type Twos often live through the affirmations of others. It's important to help them pay attention to their own needs and approach their problems with compassion.

How to Connect with Type Three?

Type Three, also known as the Achiever, seeks validation for their worth through success and admiration. Highly goal-oriented, competitive, and hard-working, they focus on achieving various goals, whether becoming the top salesperson or the most desired person in social circles. Type Threes are driven individuals who know how to set and accomplish their objectives, constantly seeking recognition and praise.

When deeply engaged in their work, Type Threes prefer to be left alone. Their pursuit of success may make relationships feel artificial and insincere, especially when they detach from the present moment and their emotions. Intimacy can be challenging at times, as their external validation masks a deep sense of shame. To connect with Type Threes, express appreciation for their achievements and ensure feedback is honest without being judgmental or overly critical.

How to Connect with Type Four?

Type Fours, known as Romantics, often experience melancholy and longing, believing that something is perpetually missing. They embark on a quest for wholeness through romantic aesthetics, healing, or idealism, convinced that lost love can be regained through fulfilling, special, and unique experiences. Despite their belief that they are too complicated or messy for society, Type Fours relentlessly pursue authentic connections.

Fueled by a desire for depth and meaning, Type Fours may be tempted to conform for acceptance while simultaneously wishing to stand out. Living in constant worry, they easily convince themselves that genuine connections are beyond their reach. Envious of others' relationships, Type Fours strive for personal creativity, meaningful work, and authentic connections in their pursuit of fulfillment.

How to Foster Harmony with Enneagram Type Five?

Enneagram type five, often referred to as the observer, is characterized by a strong inclination towards accumulating knowledge and fostering intellectual understanding. Individuals of this type are commonly recognized as technical experts or scholars due to their analytical prowess and keen perception. They exhibit a tendency to be self-reliant and private, making relationships a potentially challenging territory where expressing emotions may be difficult for them. On their best days, type fives bring valuable strengths to relationships, such as intellect, curiosity, insight, and vision. Typically thoughtful, well-read, and intelligent, they become experts in areas aligned with their interests.

For effective interaction with someone fitting this type, it's crucial to express love and respect by engaging in conversations about topics they are passionate about. Discovering and appreciating their areas of interest can lead to meaningful and enduring conversations.

How to Build a Connection with Enneagram Type Six?

Enneagram type six, also known as the questioner, is a security-oriented and committed personality. These individuals are trustworthy, responsible, hardworking, and reliable. They possess the ability to anticipate problems and foster cooperation but may sometimes become anxious, evasive, or defensive. At their best, type six individuals display courage, self-reliance, and internal stability, championing themselves and others. However, they may also become suspicious and self-questioning during challenging times.

Type six individuals employ their intellect and perception to understand the world and identify potential threats or allies. Their focus revolves around ensuring the safety of their community, project, or group, with a knack for anticipating and addressing specific problems. To connect with a type six individual, providing support, reassurance, and acknowledging their need for security is vital.

How to Cultivate a Relationship with Enneagram Type Seven?

Type sevens, known as the adventurers, make delightful co-workers, partners, and friends. They exude optimism, possess a light-hearted spirit, and are always seeking adventure. While they bring joy to relationships, sevens may struggle with confronting negative feelings, fearing their portrayal as such. In their best moments, they emanate hope and positivity, envisioning a safe world and the best in people. However, during challenges, they may become opinionated and neglect details, affecting their work and commitments.

To navigate a relationship with a type seven, it's essential to recognize their pursuit of pleasure and future-oriented mindset. While enjoying the joys they bring, one should be prepared for their occasional difficulties in facing pain and hardship, requiring support during such times.

How to Establish Understanding with Enneagram Type Eight?

Type eights, the assertors, are natural leaders who believe in taking action. They tend to assert control, actively seeking solutions, and standing up for the underdogs. Energetic and meaning-driven, type eights display generosity, playfulness, and support at their best. However, when things deviate from their expectations, they may become combative and aggressive, finding it challenging to relate to emotionally-driven individuals.

When dealing with a type eight individual, it's crucial to communicate directly and honestly. Recognizing that their assertiveness is not personal but a means of self-protection and environmental control is key. Upholding their trust, avoiding gossip, and respecting their need for space contribute to a positive interaction.

How to Foster Harmony with Enneagram Type Nine?

Type nines, known as peacemakers, are adaptable individuals often considered the chameleons of the enneagrams. They excel at relating to and adapting to other personality types, a trait that can be both a strength and a weakness. While skilled at making others feel acknowledged, they may lose their own identity in relationships.

Type nines may hold onto the belief that their opinions and presence don't matter, occasionally manifesting as passive-aggressiveness, aloofness, or distraction. However, on positive days, they can avoid conflict for connection, asserting their opinions when necessary. When interacting with type nines, inclusion in decision-making, encouraging them to voice their opinions, and providing choices in questions can enhance communication. Affirmation and celebration of their expression also contribute to a positive relationship.

24

Dynamics and Variations

The Enneagram is not ambiguous; it serves as a precise tool to identify and refine our clarity, offering a more nuanced understanding than the nine basic types. Each type is complemented by two wings and three instinctual variants, acting as lenses that enable us to focus on specific personality attributes with enhanced precision and individuality. However, what sets the Enneagram apart from other personality typologies is its ability to guide us in the most effective ways to grow. It accurately outlines the sequences of our development and identifies the patterns that may lead us into challenging situations. Through the stages of growth, integration, and disintegration, we can readily comprehend the dynamics of our personality and observe how we evolve over time.

The Wings:

The nine (more fundamental) types of the Enneagram can be individualized through the concept of wings. Each wing is essentially a subtype of the primary type. Understanding the concept of wings helps us identify the challenges we need to address on our spiritual journey. Since the nine types are arranged in a circle, regardless of your core type, there is a type on each side of it. One of the two adjacent types becomes your wing, influencing and blending with your core type, highlighting specific tendencies. For example, if your core type is nine, your wing can be either an eight-wing or a one-wing. While some individuals may exhibit traits of both wings, most people have a dominant wing. Considering the dominant wing results in a unique subtype, evident in daily life. For instance, within the seven type, you can observe individuals with an eight-wing and others with a six-wing, each presenting a distinct flavor. The various combinations of types and wings create eighteen wing subtypes, with two for each type, detailed within their respective type sections. To visualize individual differences, imagine the Enneagram's circumference as a color wheel representing the entire spectrum of available colors. The types then resemble a family of related shades, categorizing someone as, for example, part of the "blue family," indicating a six or any other type.

This perspective emphasizes a spectrum of human expression, akin to the color spectrum, with no real divisions between personality types, just as there are none between rainbow colors. Individual differences are as unique as different shades, hues, and color intensities. The nine Enneagram points serve as "family names" to discuss meaningful variations in personality, providing a way to talk about essential features without delving into intricate details.

The Instinctual Variants:

The Instinct Variants delineate which of the three basic instincts was most pronounced during one's childhood, resulting in characteristic fears and behaviors across the entire range of personality types. In addition to the two wing subtypes for each Enneagram point, there are three Instinctual Variants for each type, signifying the different life aspects where a particular type's concerns are likely to be focused. A person's dominant instinctual variant represents the arena where their type-specific issues will frequently manifest. Just as all nine Enneagram types coexist within us, all three variants do the same, with one of them usually predominating.

The three instincts – self-preservation, social, and sexual – can be ranked like layers of a cake, with the dominant instinct on top, another in the middle, and the least dominant at the bottom. This ranking occurs irrespective of the individual's Enneagram type, as instincts operate independently of type, serving as a distinct factor and not a true "subtype." These variants influence human behavior and lead to three variations for each Enneagram type based on the three possible dominant instincts. For instance, a six may be a self-preservation six, a social six, or a sexual six, each exhibiting a noticeably different set of concerns.

Consequently, an individual can be described as a combination of a core type, wing, and predominant instinctual variant. For instance, someone might be a self-preservation one with a two-wing or a sexual eight with a nine-wing. Although wings and instinctual variants are not directly related, examining a type through either the "lens" of the wing or the "lens" of the dominant instinctual variant is often more straightforward. Combining these two frames of reference yields six variations for each type, resulting in a total of fifty-four major variations in the entire Enneagram. This detailed understanding of personality dimensions may be more nuanced than some people require, but the Instinctual Variants are crucial for transformative self-awareness. Moreover, these variants play a significant role in relationships, with individuals sharing the same variant tending to have common values, while those with different variants may encounter more conflicts due to distinct core values.

Variant of Self-Preservation:

This instinctual variant is easily recognizable as individuals with self-preservation tendencies are preoccupied with acquiring and maintaining physical security and comfort. This focus often leads to concerns about food, belongings, finances, shelter, and physical well-being, making these issues a top priority. For instance, when entering a room, individuals with self-preservation tendencies immediately notice aspects related to the comfort of the environment. They quickly react to inadequate lighting, uncomfortable seating, or dissatisfaction with room temperature, continuously adjusting these elements. Questions about the next meal, coffee break, and worries about the availability and suitability of food are common. In a harmonious state, these individuals are practical and down-to-earth, channeling their energy into addressing basic life necessities such as securing a safe place, managing finances, and acquiring practical skills. However, if their personality becomes unhealthy, it distorts the self-preservation instinct, leading to poor self-care habits, potential eating and sleeping issues, and an accumulation of unnecessary possessions. While secure individuals with self-preservation tendencies may be organized and financially astute, unhealthy manifestations can result in obsessive behavior, especially regarding health and finances. The dominance of other instincts alongside a less-developed self-preservation instinct can lead to individuals neglecting fundamental life aspects, overlooking the need for proper nutrition or sufficient sleep, and disregarding environmental factors. In such cases, time and resource management are often neglected, with adverse effects on careers, social lives, and material well-being.

The Social Variant

While many of us acknowledge the presence of a social aspect in our lives, we often perceive it merely as a desire to engage in social activities, attend events, conferences, and participate in groups. However, the social instinct runs much deeper. It represents a powerful inclination inherent in all humans to seek approval, acceptance, and a sense of security in the company of others.

Individually, we are relatively fragile and susceptible, lacking the claws, fangs, and fur that protect other animals. Without coming together and collaborating, we would likely struggle to survive as a species or as individuals. The ability to adapt to others and be socially accepted is a fundamental instinct driven by the need for survival. Individuals with a dominant social instinct are preoccupied with being acknowledged and valued within their surroundings.

Their focus lies in maintaining a sense of significance derived from participating in various events, whether on a familial, corporate, community, national, or global level. Social types derive satisfaction from involvement and thrive on interactions with others for shared purposes. Upon entering a space, individuals with a social instinct immediately grasp the power dynamics and subtle interpersonal "politics" at play among different individuals and groups. They are subconsciously attuned to others' responses, particularly concerning whether they are being accepted or not.

These individuals are keenly aware of their position within a hierarchical social structure, both in relation to themselves and others. This awareness manifests in various ways, such as a desire for attention, achievement, recognition, respect, honor, leadership, and appreciation, as well as the assurance of being part of something larger than themselves. Among the various instinctual variations, social types seek to stay informed about what is happening in their world; they feel the need to connect with others to feel secure, alive, and energized. This can encompass anything from an interest in office politics or local gossip to global news and international diplomacy.

25

How to Analyze People Body Language

Exploring and decoding body language has recently become a topic of considerable discussion. It's truly remarkable! It's high time we delve into comprehending the potential power, influence, and advantages that can be harnessed when mastering non-verbal communication. However, is this the conclusion of the matter?

Numerous experts are currently offering their courses and manuals, brimming with interpretations about the specific meanings behind various non-verbal gestures. The adept ones even acknowledge that accurately interpreting most non-verbal cues requires considering the unique context or situation in which they are expressed.

Does folding your arms convey a specific message? Individuals crossing their arms could be indicating any of the following emotions:
   - Uncertainty
   - A casual attitude
   - Defensiveness
   - Aloofness
   - Confidence

A remarkably innovative and captivating leader might occasionally fold their arms to minimize the space they occupy within a group. This action has the potential to inspire more reserved individuals to express themselves more freely. However, the situation becomes more intricate when considering an uncertain person who experiences a sense of coldness but also desires to project an air of detachment.

Exploring the Meaning Behind Crossed Arms

A significant portion of the puzzle that constitutes Body Language remains undiscovered, as indicated by various accounts. The mastery of Conscious Body Language may be the key to unraveling this enigma. While one can learn to identify and analyze every signal and subtle expression, similar capabilities can be achieved by a biometric computer. However, without developing a sense of understanding and emotion regarding the dynamics within both oneself and others, one may still miss the point. Consequences may range from a failed business deal to a breach of trust or a child's emotional distress, even if one appears correct based on literature.

Enhancing both your ability and intuition to "feel" the unique context and nuances of the communicated body language opens up an entirely new realm of possibilities. This involves recognizing "The Issue in the Tissue." Could this be the missing link in how humans can better communicate, connect, and thrive together?

For the Sake of Harmony, Imagine a World without Interruption

Envision a world where everyone is raised to perceive and respect each other's boundaries – a reality where we learn to seek permission before entering personal spaces. The trend of "permission marketing" is gaining momentum online. Why not continue expanding our understanding to include such respectful practices in face-to-face interactions?

Decoding Body Language in Face-to-Face Communication

It's likely you've already discovered that humans don't universally react, respond, or behave in the same way. Understanding common interpretations of certain body language gestures can certainly guide you. However, without consulting a real-time guide specific to the individual in front of you, how can you be certain of the accurate interpretation? Navigating the timely process of finding the right page in your manual and aligning it with your audience's manual is no easy task. Here, some of our Sensational Soft Skills can be incredibly useful, including:
  - Being present
  - Breathing for inspiration
  - Listening with all your senses
  - Trusting and following your instincts
  - Being open, inquisitive, and vulnerable
  - Recognizing thoughts and feelings from your head, heart, and "gut."

Whether you're leading, selling, serving customers, team-building, or simply aiming to improve your well-being or relationships, employing conscious non-verbal communication can enhance your understanding of the situation. These soft skills can complement the body language courses and training you've undertaken, collectively unlocking new dimensions in personal communication.

Mastering the Art of Interpreting Body Language

It's a fact that sometimes what people say differs from what they truly think or feel. The reverse is also true – your body language influences what others perceive about you, so it's crucial not to send the wrong signals. We all use body language signals to reinforce our words and emotions, whether consciously or subconsciously. These postures, intentional or automatic, invariably reflect the strengths and weaknesses of our characters. Hence, it's important to bear in mind that as we decode the body language of others, they are simultaneously interpreting our body language signals, both intentionally and unintentionally.

Detecting Warning Signs

Many of the emotions we experience when evaluating individuals are subconscious assessments. The way we interpret someone's non-verbal cues plays a crucial role in the feelings we form about them. If you've ever questioned someone you don't really know, there's likely something in that person's body language that has triggered red flags.

Even when employing deliberate gestures during communication, it's essential to use body language that feels natural. You don't want to come across as rehearsed. Any conscious effort you put into your body language should be aimed at avoiding gestures that may convey unfavorable messages about your character. Fortunately, authentic body language naturally emerges when we strive to be ourselves. The key is to exude confidence and relaxation. If you feel at ease, others are likely to feel comfortable in your presence.

Individuals projecting positive body language signals walk with their heads up and shoulders back—an erect posture signaling confidence. Establishing and maintaining eye contact during conversation fosters trust. When walking or sitting, keep your arms relaxed at your sides with open palms. Others naturally interpret these postures as a sign of your approachability and trustworthiness.

First-Time Meetings

When meeting someone for the first time, avoid adopting a neutral or defensive posture. If standing in a particular way boosts your confidence, take that stance to appear more self-assured. Expanding the space around you makes you appear larger, conveying confidence and importance.

Offering a genuine smile is one of the best ways to make others feel at ease in your presence. Ensure that your smile reaches beyond your lips for others to believe it is sincere. A reassuring smile goes a long way in comforting others, but if it seems forced, it may induce nervousness in them.

When shaking hands, ensure a firm grip without being overly forceful. You want to convey confidence and sincerity without appearing domineering. Respect personal space boundaries, especially with individuals you've just met. As familiarity grows, you'll become more attuned to their typical body language, aiding in recognizing shifts in mood or attitude.

Even your breathing can exhibit positive non-verbal communication. Taking slow, deep breaths helps reduce anxiety, particularly in first-time encounters. Rather than appearing nervous and tense, aim to exude a carefree demeanor.

Understanding Eye Movements

When interpreting body language, paying attention to the eyes is crucial. Eyes convey a wealth of information about an individual, including their thought processes. Observing the direction, size of pupils, and eye movement provides valuable insights.

Looking upward indicates thinking in images, while looking toward the ears suggests contemplation of a sound. A downward gaze signifies emotional processing. Additionally, pay attention to the lateral eye movement; looking to the left may indicate logical thinking, while looking to the upper right suggests recalling visual memories. Interpretations vary, so avoid jumping to conclusions when reading eye movements.

In body language analysis, consider eye movements alongside other non-verbal cues, treating them like words in a sentence. The duration of eye contact during a conversation also holds significance, conveying feelings of approval, interest, desire for conversation, or internal preoccupation. To decipher the meaning behind different gazes, rely not only on eye movements but also on overall body language and attentive listening. Additionally, pupil size can offer insights, provided the lighting is appropriate, and the person is not under the influence of substances altering pupil size.

Conclusion

Our lives are profoundly influenced by an invisible force—the subconscious. Acting like an unseen compass, it plays a pivotal role in shaping our existence, often making critical decisions on our behalf. While we may believe that our choices are entirely our own, many are, in fact, products of our subconscious conditioning. Our minds navigate decisions based on core values, expectations, and the environmental influences we encounter.

Understanding what brings us joy and recognizing what we wish to avoid, even if it brings sadness, is crucial. Yet, despite this self-awareness, we may find ourselves in unfamiliar emotional territories, struggling to comprehend the reasons behind our discontent.

The Enneagram serves as a valuable tool in addressing profound questions that often elude us. By identifying personality types and aligning them with our daily decision-making patterns, we gain insights into what truly motivates and defines us. Our personalities, far from developing solely in maturity, are shaped by early experiences, relationships, and the environments we engage with—from loved ones to school lessons and community influences.

As we age, we become acutely aware of our imperfections, recognizing the distinctions between ourselves and others. Our varied approaches to similar situations become apparent, manifesting our unique personalities shaped by a lifetime of experiences.

The Enneagram, a centuries-old method, unveils nine distinct personality types within us. While one may dominate, others subtly influence us, especially under specific circumstances. Self-awareness, a crucial step in personal growth, reveals truths about ourselves, helping us address insecurities that may otherwise remain hidden.

This guide walks through each personality type, outlining general characteristics that serve as starting points. Further classifications delve into the manifestation of behaviors in actions, thoughts, and feelings. By focusing on these elements, we cultivate fundamental self-awareness, enabling us to confront unexplained thoughts and emotions that complicate our lives.

Insecurities, often dealt with through avoidance or projection onto others, can be overcome with an understanding of our personality types. Acceptance of ourselves, imperfections included, empowers us to lead fulfilling lives, acknowledging inhibitions and devising strategies to compensate for them.

The wisdom embedded in the Enneagram extends beyond self-acceptance, aiding us in comprehending core beliefs and shaping our worldview. A balanced life, though challenging, becomes attainable when we unlock our potential by understanding our personality type and utilizing it in our interactions.

Embarking on the journey of self-discovery requires time and patience. The rewards, however, promise a life that is spiritually uplifting and deeply satisfying once we grasp the profound impact of our personalities on our experiences and relationships.

www.ingramcontent.com/pod-product-compliance
Lightning Source LLC
LaVergne TN
LVHW012000070526
838202LV00054B/4979